How to Be a Cocktail Waitress and Make Big Tips

Simple money-making strategies for the new cocktail waitress

Romana Van Lissum

Romana Van Lissum

Copyright © 2015 by Romana Van Lissum

Published by: Anamor Publishing
Canadian Address
Box 19, Station Whonnock
Maple Ridge, BC, Canada
V2W 1V9

Romana can be contacted at romana@howtobeawaitress.com

All Rights Reserved, including the right to reproduce this book in any form whatsoever, including digital, without permission in writing from the publisher, except for brief passages in connection with a review.

Unauthorized duplication or distribution is strictly prohibited.

Notice of Liability: The information in this book is distributed on an "as is" basis, without warranty. While every precaution has been taken in the preparation of this book, neither the author or the publisher shall have any liability to any person or entity with respect to any liability, loss, or damage caused or alleged to be caused directly or indirectly by the instructions contained in this book.

Dedication

This book is dedicated to all the new waitresses I have had the honour of training and help mold into the fantastic servers they are today.

Romana Van Lissum

Table of Contents

About This Book 1

Chapter 1 - The Cocktail Waitress 3

Top Cocktail Waitress Qualities. 4
The Downside to Cocktail Waitressing 5
A Typical Shift in the Day of a Cocktail Waitress 6
How to Make Yourself the TOP Earner. 17
Care of the Cocktail Waitress on the Inside and Out 20
Tips to Become a Well-Rounded Cocktail Server. 25
Important Safety Tips at Your Job 30
What to Do In Case of an Attack. 35
Server Sign Language Signals 38

Chapter 2 - Selling .41

Bar Lingo / Terminology 41
Sales Strategies 46
A Little Secret to Making Extra Money 49
Important Tips for Running Tabs. 51
Securing a Tip 61
The "Art" of Handing Back Change 66
Promotions, Celebrations and Special Events 74

Chapter 3 - Organization in the Cocktail Waitress's World 79

The Cocktail Waitress Tool Kit 79
The Ways You Can Protect Yourself From Losing Money 86
The Fundamentals of Counting Money. 95
The Memorizing Secret 98

Chapter 4 - Different Strategies of Speed 105
A Typical Slammed Night For a Cocktail Waitress 105
Manage Your Time Efficiently 111
Saving Time 113
What to Do if You Forget a Drink 115

Chapter 5 - Downtime. 119
Helping Coworkers 119
Preparation for the Busy Shifts 121
Tipping out Fellow Servers 127
Cleanliness 129

Chapter 6 - The Different Types of Customers 133
The "Regular" Customer 133
The "Creep" 138
The Player 143
The Friend 143
Women 144
The Kids 145
The Bad Boys 150
The Rude Customer 151
The "No Manners" Customer. 153
The Jerk. 154
The High Maintenance Customer 155
The Drunk 156

Chapter 7 - The Cocktail Waitress Tray and Money 161
Holding, Arranging and Balancing Your Tray 161
Cash Caddy vs. Ashtray. 169
How to Correctly Hold Your Paper Money in Your Fingers. . . . 172
Inspecting Bills for Fakes 174
Did you know…?. 176

Chapter 8 - The Downside of Serving 183
The Bar Rules. 183
The Dreaded Price Increase 186
It Sucks to Get Stiffed 187
Serving It Right and Other Mandatory Self-study Courses 188
Asking Customers for Identification 188
Dealing With Problem Customers 193
Cutting Patrons Off 194
Problems with Coworkers. 197
Other Problems with Customers 199
What to Do if a Customer Won't Leave When You Ask Him To . . 202
Dumb Things People Say and How to Deal With It 203
Action Steps to a Dine and Dash 210

Bonus - Why Men Like To Hang Out in Strip Bars 213

About the Author 219

Romana Van Lissum

About This Book

I have been a cocktail waitress working for the same strip bar in the Greater Vancouver area for over 20 years. There are many reasons as to why I've been there for so long. I love the staff, the customers, and the hours, it's close to my home and of course, I love the money!

I have probably met almost every type of personality out there and I've had many different serving experiences. Some were upsetting and threw a hiccup into my shift, but I managed to make it through each one and learn from them all. As I think about a bad situation, sometimes I realize I could have handled it in a more positive way and other times they were just bad situations I really had not much control in. It was an unfortunate circumstance I just happened to experience on my shift and in the end I learned from it. Waitressing is a job where you're always undergoing new situations. You're dealing with the public and this can be extremely challenging at times.

This book is the outcome of many experiences I've dealt with over the last 20 years as a cocktail waitress in a strip bar. This knowledge is turned into advice I wanted to dissect and put into a very thorough, easy-to-understand format. I wanted to put a book together which was helpful for all waitresses encountering many different obstacles in our profession; from the newbie who's never held a tray, to the old pro who still likes to learn new tricks now and then. I want this book to be picked up by an individual who has never worked in our industry and for them to have a clear understanding of what it takes to do this job. Learning to use a till and getting the hang of balancing a full tray of drinks is the easy part. It's the 'not knowing how to deal with intoxicated customers,' being left with unpaid tabs and a customer who won't take, "No, I will not go out with you. I told you I'm married for the fifth time!" are a few of the annoyances a waitress has to deal with.

Although there are concerning aspects to the job, I'm going to show you how to deal with most of them so you are fully aware and prepared for what may lie ahead. This job has been fun, challenging, and very profitable, and I want to show you how to have the same things.

As you read this book, most of the time I will be referring to the term '*server*', which is a modern definition for waitress or waiter which is used in the industry today. To simplify and shorten my writing even further, I will refer to a server as '*she*', a female. Since I work in a gentleman's club and most of my clientele are men, I will be referring to customers as '*he*', the male. The information in this book is geared towards serving men but is helpful to all servers who serve men and women in *any* serving establishment.

Use your best judgment and always ask a senior server about house policies on running tabs and other important aspects of the job since every establishment has its own policies and rules.

Over the 20 years of serving, I figured out how to deal with most problems on my own if I didn't have the advice or help from others. Every server is different and the more you work and the more of an expert you become in this industry, you will feel out certain situations and figure out what will work for you and what will not.

Working in this business is enjoyable and very profitable. I can't imagine a better job where I can make the money I do, meet some great people on a daily basis and have the fun I have.

If you decide to enter the serving industry, read this book and refer to it many times. Take what you want from it and leave the rest. As a result, I want you to enjoy your road traveled in this interesting profession and make lots of money.

Romana Van Lissum
www.howtobeawaitress.com

Chapter 1
The Cocktail Waitress

Many people may wonder why a person wants to get into the crazy profession of cocktail waitressing. Some of the shifts can be long and crazy, you work weekends and holidays, you're on your feet at all times, you get hit on, you're dealing with a high-paced job and there are many different personalities you encounter.

Cocktail waitressing is a hard job, but it's very rewarding as well. You meet some great people, the hours can fit into almost any person's schedule and the money can be pretty damn good!

It's great to go home at the end of a shift with instant cash in your pocket, so there's always money for gas or a loaf of bread. Plus, you still get a pay cheque every couple of weeks.

When the economy is down and people are losing their jobs, you'll find bars are still busy as ever because when times get tough, people will always drink. When times are good, people will drink to celebrate as well. The hospitality industry rarely will get affected as people will drink when they are happy and when they are sad.

Many people turn to cocktail serving because of the hours. If you look around, you will be able to find a pub, nightclub, strip bar or anywhere else serving alcohol during the hours you need to make some extra money.

Some girls think they'll do it for a few years and then move on to something else, while other girls end up enjoying the hours, the people and the money. They never leave the industry, like me, and turn into a career waitress.

Professional men and women work office jobs by day and turn to serving at night for extra cash. Single mothers raise their families on the money they make waitressing and then have the day to spend with their children. Students go to school during the day and waitress at night to help pay their way through school.

You don't need to take a course or get a degree to learn how to be a waitress. If you enjoy people, are organized, enjoy a fast-paced work environment and love cash, this is the industry to get involved in.

For most of my serving years, I've enjoyed working the nightshift, so my daughter didn't have to be raised by a babysitter and I was able to train my horses during the day. It was a bit of a crazy schedule for my husband and me, as our only day off together was Sunday for many years. Eventually, we both ended up with Sundays and Mondays as our days off together. Many of our friends and family were amazed our marriage was strong enough to withstand the crazy bar hours I worked.

Looking at our vast industry, you will see that cocktail servers are needed for many businesses. You'll find cocktail servers in nightclubs, pubs, gentlemen's clubs, beer gardens, piano bars, cruise ships, golf courses and casinos. Not only do cocktail waitresses serve alcoholic and non-alcoholic beverages, some also serve pub food.

Top Cocktail Waitress Qualities

The amount of money a server makes depends on a few things. You have to have a talent for this type of work and it helps to be outgoing, quick thinking and have a lot of stamina.

You can't be intimidated to go up to a big group of people and take over the situation. You may have a loudmouth in the group and a snotty wife darting dirty looks at you. You have to stay on top of your game, take their orders and keep a smile on your face while you feel like kicking the loudmouth in the shin and dumping your tray of drinks in the lap of the snotty wife.

Quick-thinking girls know how to handle vulgar comments while memorizing a full tray of drinks. They keep on top of checking identification of the young-looking clientele and keeping a tidy and orderly room all at the same time.

The stamina comes in handy when the bar is full of people and you must keep running out with a full tray after full tray of drinks while returning back to the bar with a tray of empties and not skipping a beat. You may be weaving and fighting your way through a crowd of people, while avoiding the drunks and keeping them from crashing into your tray. Sometimes there's no stopping for a breather. You barely have a moment to sip some water and sometimes you have to wait a while before you have a minute to slip into the restroom.

Unorganized, shy people who get flustered easily don't last long in this job.

Another advantage to serving is that since you deal with cash most of your shift, you will end up with collector's coins and money from around the world. I have one hell of a big coin collection.

The Downside to Cocktail Waitressing

As with everything, there are some disadvantages to this line of work. When you're the new person, you will usually get the hours which are the shortest and during the slower times. When you come in for a shift and it's not busy, you may have to sit on the side lines and wait until the room picks up. Sometimes it never does and during the dead nights you may not end up working at all. It's silly to put another server on the floor and pay her an hourly wage when there are not even twenty drinkers in the room. I feel bad when I tell a new server to sit and wait, but that's the way it is. As senior waitress, you have to make good business decisions that are advantageous to the bar. When you're new, you will usually be given the section of the room that is perhaps smaller than and not as busy as the other servers'.

In this line of work, you will also encounter the unruly customer and the person who commands attention by either starting a fight or yelling. They may have been cut off in another bar and unfortunately ended up at yours. You'll have to cut people off if they've had too much to drink and babysit them until their safe ride shows up.

Non-tippers who expect you to get their drinks for them all night long without compensating you with a tip are a few of the people who will make you cringe.

You'll be looked upon as eye candy, especially if you're very attractive or working in a strip bar. Believe me, there are days you won't be in the mood for it but it comes with the territory.

There is a reason why I like working in a room full of men: some women are difficult to deal with. The jealous female is the worst. Just because I serve men in a strip bar doesn't mean I'm there to pick guys up and take them home. I have my own at home that I am very happy with… thank you very much!

You have to be safe and aware of your surroundings as you leave the bar late at night while going out to your car. You don't know who you will meet while serving during your shift. I've met my share of weirdos and the last thing I want is for some unstable nut following me home.

Another disadvantage is that you can get caught up in the drinking and socializing aspect of this job because it's entertaining and fun. It's very tempting and in the beginning, I got roped into it like many do.

There is no shame in being a career waitress. I can definitely say it has been a fun job I find very fulfilling and I wouldn't trade it for another. I would suggest going to school and getting some sort of a degree while making money in this field because one day you'll feel the pressure of not being the hot, young girl anymore. You really can't be doing this job when you're an old timer because it's very demanding on your body. A big dilemma to being a career waitress is you may have trouble with banks since they only look at your wage and not include the tips you've earned to get a loan.

A Typical Shift in the Day of a Cocktail Waitress

I would like to give you a taste of a typical shift and the approach to serving customers. I'll go into greater detail later in other chapters.

I like to arrive at work at least fifteen minutes early since this will give me enough time to change into my work clothes and proper footwear. This is the time to use the toilet if I need to and re-apply my lipstick. (If you think you may be a few minutes late, always call the bar and let them know but don't get into the habit of running late very often).

When I collect my tray, I give it a quick clean if it feels dirty, feels sticky or smells bad. Our trays are lined with cork and we find that sprinkling a bit of baking soda and some hot water on them, then rubbing the baking soda in with the top side of a glass gets rid of the stink from the shift before. Baking soda is fantastic to use on all trays to clean them. Trays with a rubber coating can be run through the glass washer.

I like to have my own float but most girls borrow theirs from the bartender. A float is money in bills and coin lent to a server to use as change and it's paid back to the bar before the end of the shift. Every server seems to like a different float. The standard float at our bar is a roll of nickels (two dollars), a roll of quarters (ten dollars), a roll of loonies (twenty five dollars), three loonies (three dollars) and four fives (twenty dollars). This equals sixty dollars. We don't bother with dimes as they're a waste of space on our tray and dealing with nickels is a lot easier anyways. You also don't have to waste your time by counting and rolling up dimes at the end of your shift. If you borrow your float from the bar, write a note to yourself that you owe the bartender $60.00 (or whatever amount you borrow) for your float and slip it into your waitress box. This way, if he forgets to collect from you, you would know beforehand and not go home at the end of your shift thinking you were $60.00 richer than you actually were. You would be expected to pay your float back next time you come in for a shift.

I wet my rag and fold it neatly, placing it on top of my coins arranged in my ashtray. This way, my change is hidden and basically the only thing taking up any room on my tray is the ashtray. If I'm using my cash caddy that shift, I place my wet rag beside it).

If I'm relieving another server at the end of her shift, I'll ask her how the day went and if anything interesting is going on in the bar. This is the time she'll let me know of patrons who are cut off, any tabs owing to her, stag or birthday parties in the room, etc.

If I feel anxious or seem to be in a bad mood, I SNAP OUT OF IT QUICK! People will feel your energy and read your body language. Customers have come into your bar to relax and have a good time, and nobody likes to be served by a crab who has a scowl on her face and barely utters a "Hello." Personally, I would sooner tip a server who is friendly and slow to bring my drinks than a crabby speed bomb who looks like she hates her job.

Onto the floor I go. As I walk through the room, I make sure to smile and greet every single customer and ask how they're doing tonight. During the entire time I'm working the floor, I'm picking up empties, wiping tables and pushing chairs in. This is all very important as it makes the room look clean and neat. If you stay in the habit, it's easy and quick to do. I could never understand servers who would rather trip through or walk around chairs, rather than push them under the table and get them out of the way.

Always remove all empties and garbage as soon as possible when a group has paid their bill and left to go home. If the table is cluttered with empties, newcomers entering the room will think the table is being used and the occupants are outside having a cigarette or in the restroom. You could be deterring potential customers from sitting in your section by not clearing dirty tables right away. *Having people in all your seats means you're maximizing your section and making money!*

When picking up empties from a table, I always give the spot it was sitting on a quick wipe to get rid of the sticky or wet ring with my damp cloth. The only exception would be if I'm slammed and I can barely keep up to collecting empties in the room. Wiping can be done when I swing by the next time I run by. Selling drinks should be your number one task to do.

As I move through the room taking orders, I keep a look-out for accidental spills or empties. As I'm removing the empties or wiping up the spill, I'll mention to the customer, "Let me get rid of the evidence for you!" I always have guys laughing when I make this silly comment to them. It shows your playful and fun side which may increase your tips.

You don't have to have a fake smile plastered on your face as you mechanically go about your job. You want to look like you're having fun there too. If you're having fun and enjoying your job, your smile will be sincere.

Another fun comment that makes the guys smile is when I drop off a round of drinks. They say, "Thank you," and I respond with, "Thank you for keeping me busy!" It's entertaining to be a goof! When you make people feel good and have fun, they'll tip you for it.

Try to get in the habit of placing coasters under every drink. It keeps the table dry and saves on your clean up later. Our bar keeps pint glasses in a cooler so when draft beer is poured, it is icy cold. Customers are especially grateful for this in the hot summer months. Ice may be clumped at the bottom when the pint is set down, resulting in the icy mug almost sliding into a customer's lap. Keep those coasters handy and pay attention if there is ice accumulated at the bottom of the pint. I will either chip the ice away with a bottle opener or bang the glass firmly on the counter to break off the ice.

As I move around the room and clean my tables, there may be change left on a table I didn't serve. That tip doesn't belong to me but it does go to the server who was just working. I leave it in her box or take it to her if she's still in the room. You want to be honest as Karma will follow you. Let me assure you that cheaters and stealers won't last long in this business.

Make that Sale

As I move through the room, I'm scanning every single drink on every single table. If the drink is half full or less, I'll ask that customer if they're ready for another. This is an opportunity to make a sale and possibly a tip.

When I take new drink orders and a cocktail or high ball is ordered, I ask the customer if they want to double it up; think higher sales for the bar and a possible bigger tip for you!

I'm also looking for customers who are flagging me down by waving their hand at me or if they have that longing look in their eyes. You know "the look"… when you walk over and ask, "Did you need another beer?" and with their three-quarter-full beer in their hand they answer with a nod and sigh, "Yes, please!" He's the customer who will be done by the time you swing by with his next drink. He's either very thirsty or in a rush to down a few beers and take off.

I'd like to comment about enunciation and hearing. When a customer is giving you his order and you can't hear him, say "I'm sorry, I can't hear you!" If you still can't hear, don't be shy to repeat yourself. It's happened a few times where someone will order a Kokanee, and I thought I heard "coke." I don't happen to pick up "anee" at the end and end up bringing a coke. I apologize and tell him my hearing is really bad from working in the bar for so long. Bud vs. mug is another one. If a customer says "Bud," I'll repeat back with "Budweiser?" just to be clear.

Always stick to a pattern or map of the room. You don't want to wander the room aimlessly and miss people sitting at a table in a dark corner. You'll make them mad since it looks like you're avoiding them. You'll also be missing out on valuable sales and possible tips for yourself!

When I return to the bar, I unload my empties while waiting for any other servers or shooter girls to finish with the till. If there is no room for me, with my tray on my arm I remove the empties and garbage. This way, I make use of valuable time and I can sort out the drink order I have memorized in my head. I don't waste my time and stand there waiting for the other servers to get out of the way. I set my tray down and help her unload her tray while she rings in her order so it can speed everyone up at the till.

I make sure to always dump any little bit of beer at the bottom of beer bottles, as well as ice in glasses into the sink. The reason for the beer bottles to be empty is that when you lift the beer case full of empties and if it happens to drop suddenly, you don't get splashed in the face or your shirt with old, stale beer. Take it from a girl who knows. The bartenders and beer delivery guys appreciate this courtesy as well since they are the ones moving those cases around.

DO NOT slam empty bottles into the case, place them in gently. I've been in a real rush at times and don't pay attention to this warning, only to get pieces of glass flying out nearly hitting my eyes!

Keep water by the till and sip on it regularly throughout your shift. I find this very important because if I don't, I end up with a headache. My husband says I don't seem to have that thirst mechanism in my body to tell me when I'm thirsty. He's right, since I can work in the hot sun for three hours without feeling thirsty and then wonder why my head hurts a short time later. So, I make it a point to always keep a drink for myself at the till to keep hydrated.

The Drink Order

During a slower dayshift, the bartender may be doing other chores than just standing around. There are garnishes to be cut, cleaning, restocking and inventory control. If he's busy doing something with his back facing you or he's in the back room, I like to ring my order in and call loudly, "Order up!" This is an indication that I'm waiting for him to make my drink order.

When punching a drink order in, there is always an order to punching your drinks into the till. Check with your head waitress or bartender for the order in which they'd like you to ring your drinks in. If you have a newer till system, it may categorize your drinks in a particular order for you but if you have an old system, you'll have to do it manually.

At the bar I work at, we ring in our drinks in this order:

- Import beers
- Local beers
- Coolers and ciders
- Bottles of water
- Single high balls, then doubles
- Single cocktails, then doubles
- Shooters (if there's no shooter girl on)

- Pops, juices, and coffees
- Jugs
- Pints
- Sleeves

Try to ring everything in order. It can make a bartender leap over the bar for your throat if you ring in orders like this:

- Rum coke
- Stella
- Budweiser
- Double Caesar
- Budweiser
- Jug of dark
- Budweiser
- Bombay tonic
- Pineapple juice
- Miller

The reason why drinks are rung into the till in sequence is to save time. When the bartender looks at the order and starts pulling bottles of beer out of the cooler, he wants to pull out all three Budweisers and the Stella at once. He wastes time if he pulls bottles onto the counter and then has to turn around and open and shut the cooler doors again if he needs to go back in a few more times. I get very upset at servers who do this because I'm waiting my turn to get my drink order and if another server makes me wait longer than necessary, it reflects on the tips I receive!

At my bar, we are told to memorize all drink orders rather than writing them down because it saves time. Yes, you may forget a drink or two or maybe even three. This will happen when you're slammed and feel like you're starting to get out of control. You know what?

You're only human! Just apologize, get those forgotten drinks and move on. If you find you're starting to get flustered and you need to pull yourself together, move to the side and let the server behind you into the till. I find that retracing my steps and looking back at the room helps a lot.

Have a System for Identifying Your Drinks

As your bartender is working on your order, begin placing your drinks on your tray while putting garnishes and straws into them. He'll make the drinks in order of the way you rang your order in (usually from your right to the left). Always ask the bartender, as each one may have his own system of making drinks.

Always have a plan for marking the drinks on your tray.

Example:

If I have an order that calls for two Caesars, one with no Tabasco, I put two straws into the Caesar with no Tabasco.

If I have an order that calls for a Jack Daniels coke, Rum coke, Vodka coke, and a Vodka diet, I'll arrange my drinks like this… I put two straws into the Jack Daniels, a lime twist goes straight into my rum, the vodka has the lime twist sitting on the rim of the glass and the vodka diet has two straws with the lime twist sitting on the rim of the glass too. To arrange the drinks, I keep them in an alphabetical order…starting at the left side of my tray I place the Jack Daniels, beside it to the right will be the rum, to the right of that will be the vodka coke and to the right of that will be the vodka diet. My bottles and everything else will be set in the remaining space.

If I have a whole slew of cocktails, I use any system to keep it all organized. If my entire tray is full of cocktails with coke mix, I will even put three straws into a drink to be able to recognize it. I'll put my drinks in alphabetical order as well, with two straws signifying a double short. Whatever system you use to keep drinks recognized, use it. If you put two or three straws into a drink to keep your drinks organized, always remove the extra straws before setting it down in front of your customer.

As your bartender makes your drinks, do not wander away to talk to customers or go to the bathroom. This is irritating for other servers who are trying to juggle their tray and get their drink orders too.

Some old school bars may still use the call order system. This is where the server calls all her drinks out to the bartender. Look towards the bartender when you call your drinks. Stay a few drinks ahead, as you call loud and not too fast. Don't rattle off the long list as fast as you can. He needs to register in his mind what you are calling out.

If you mix up a couple of drinks, you can still save the situation and switch them if both people didn't drink out of them. If one person sips out of his drink and then complains to you, wait to see if the other person says anything. Most of the time, people won't notice anyways and you'll just have to replace only one drink instead of two. For example, customer A at table #12 orders a rye coke and customer B at table #13 orders a rum coke. When dropping off the drinks, you accidentally gave customer A the rum and customer B received the rye.

When grabbing straws to place into your drinks, don't touch them by the end where the customer places his lips. Instead, grab it at the middle. Our hands are extremely unsanitary as we are consistently handling coin, bills, garbage and empties while touching others' hands. Keep hands away from your face and wash or sanitize your hands as often as you remember. Imagine how many germs are on the mouth end of an empty beer bottle!

Some of my regulars prefer to have a cold frosty mug to go alongside their bottle of beer. I like to take it one step further and pour the contents of their bottle into the glass and deliver it that way. It saves room on my tray, keeps the table from getting more cluttered and they love the extra special touch that I provide.

Take the frosty glass and give the interior a quick rinse with water before you pour the contents of the bottle into it. This keeps the beer from foaming and spilling over the glass. Tip the glass on its side and pour the beer slowly from the bottle onto the side of the glass. It'll keep the beer from overflowing the glass and foaming like crazy.

When your tray is ready to go and you still need to sign out a tab, move your tray off to the side to do this as to keep out of the way of other servers.

Before I deliver the cheque to my customer, I will always finalize it with:

Cheers! Romana. The reason I do this is to make it more personable and I want them to know my name. So, next time they come in, they'll ask for me by name. (Or better yet, maybe they want to get hold of management and tell them they had the most awesome server ever named Romana and she needs a raise!)

As I return to the floor, I stay on the map of the room (or my section, if I'm working with another server), so as not to miss anyone. I stop at my first table and start setting down drinks. At this time I say, "There you go guys. Is that all together or separate?" At this point someone may offer me a credit card to run a tab or money will be pulled out by individuals to pay for their drinks separately.

Remember your manners and always say "Thank you," whether you receive a tip or not. Keep in mind they may still leave money on the table before they leave.

When I stop at a table and set down a pint of draft beer, sometimes a customer will have a small amount of beer at the bottom of the last purchased pint. Do not dump the leftover into the fresh one without asking him if it's okay to do this. Some guys won't drink the rest and want it taken away. When I was new to the business, I was trying to be really efficient. I grabbed a customer's pint with the little bit of draft leftover and quickly poured it into the new one I had just placed down for him. He was not happy and told me to never do that without asking again. I was embarrassed and learned my lesson then and there. From that day forward, I always ask before I pull a move like that again.

When picking up empty beer bottles, give the bottle a small shake to tell whether there is any beer still left at the bottom. I have been chased across the bar by a customer a few times who complained he still had a sip full of beer left.

When customers leave for the night, I will always call over at them with a "Thanks for coming in, guys!" or "Thanks a lot, guys! Have a great evening!" or "Enjoy the rest of your day, guys!" When you work at a bar long enough and get to know many regulars, don't be surprised if customers come over to hug you or kiss your hand or cheek as they say their good byes.

When customers leave, I run over as soon as I can and take away all the empties and garbage, straighten and wipe down the table and push in all the chairs. This clean and neat table looks inviting to a new group of people who enter the bar. New customers scan the room for a place to sit and will want to sit at a clean table. I like to keep all my tables more inviting than my coworkers' because this will keep bodies in the chairs in my section, which means my sales are high and I earn more tips.

As I near the end of a shift, I make sure I don't have any drinks I had ordered earlier and couldn't sell, sitting on ice. I'll collect any open drinks and try to sell them since the bar can't recap opened beers.

As customers leave the bar, always thank them for coming in and tell them to have a great night or rest of the day. Pick up all your empties and all garbage. We like to spray down all of our tables with a cleaner to get rid of all spills and stickiness at the end of the night. You will want to find out what cleaning protocol is from your senior servers at your bar. You will also find out what to do with the chairs and bar stools. Are they pushed in or set upside down on the tables so the room is ready for the cleaning people?

All cases full of empty bottles are stored away, the sink is cleaned out and scrubbed, and the till area is cleaned up and wiped down. The servers clean their trays and put them away. All dirty rags are put in a bucket for the cleaning people to take away and wash. As you run all dirty glass wear through the glass washer, add the bar mats and tools the bartender puts onto the counter as well.

The Structure of Cash-out

You'll want to take directions on your bar's cash-out. The following is our procedure.

Check if you have any voids to ring in. Ask the coworker responsible to do this.

Do your ring-out. This is the total amount of drinks you rang in during the course of your shift. Grab your calculator, pen, cash-out paper and envelope. Pull out all credit card and interac slips, cash, promo cards and anything else you need out of your waitress box. Do a thorough check of your box so a slip or bill is not hiding up in a corner. Make sure to do a ring-out total for your visa and interac slips as well.

As you add all your totals, always double check all calculations. If the numbers don't match up, do a third and even fourth tally if you have to. Don't be in a rush to run out the door. Make sure your cash is bang on. Remember to put money aside for your DJ, doorman, kitchen and especially your wonderful bartender; if it wasn't for him, you wouldn't be able to get your drinks out quickly to your customers (who in turn leave you a big tip!).

Before I leave for the night, I print off an extra copy of my ring-out for that shift and slip it into my waitress bag. Once in a while the till isn't cleared to zero from the day before, so when you print off your sales for a shift and the numbers look a lot higher than normal, you have your correct total from the day before to deduct from.

How to Make Yourself the TOP Earner

Out of all the chapters in this book, this is one of the most lengthy. There are a few points covered here which are repeated in detail in other chapters. I just had many points to cover and it all seemed to roll together.

I must be doing something right when every boss I've had, seems to push the new girl at me and says to her, "Romana's going to train you. Do what Ro does." I'm proud of the fact that I am good at my job and others see this as well.

An acronym to keep in mind…

Every Successful Server Needs S.H.O.E.S.

Smile
Honesty
Organization
Enthusiasm/Energy
Sexuality (your persona, your self-carriage, and the way you dress)

I'll explain in detail throughout the book as to why these characteristics are important in this line of work.

Do Not Lie to Get the Job.

You picked this book and you're reading it for a reason. Perhaps you're a girl or guy who has always wondered about the cocktail serving industry, thinking you would enjoy it and heard about the great money cocktail servers make. Maybe you're a rookie server who feels she needs to learn a few tricks to get more skilled at her job. Perhaps you're the old pro who's curious if there's anything different or new to learn. Use the tricks in this book and it'll slowly change you into a more efficient and profitable server!

Please don't think by reading this book (or any other serving book) you can lie to get a job by saying you have experience serving, when in fact you have absolutely none. You'll be caught within the first few minutes on the job. It's unfair for the girl who's supposed to train you or work with you and it's unfair to the customers you serve.

To become a good server, you need to know how to multi-task. Exposure to all sorts of scenarios and people will help over the years, as well as learning the basics, understanding and working the till and then basically being thrown to the wolves for the experience.

Cocktail waitressing can be very fast-paced and confusing at times. By the time you memorize a large table's confusing drink order, three people decide to order something completely different or a table decided to separate their bill after all. You're under pressure, but if you've got it under control, your speed is bang on and you're moving along efficiently—it's a great feeling!

Your Cocktail Waitress Resume

Here's a story for you to digest…

Around the same time I got into serving, my husband got laid off as an auto mechanic at the dealership he worked at. As he looked for another job, he dropped his résumé off at six different dealerships he wanted to work at. Three days later he got a call from our local Toyota dealership and got the job.

Years later, he was told by the manager they had a big stack of résumés around the time he got hired. The reason he got hired was he put something on his cover sheet nobody else did and it showed his desire to work there. In his résumé, he stated he would work for free for two weeks to prove himself to let them judge if he was a good enough mechanic or not to hire on. Regardless, he got paid from the day he was hired almost twenty years ago. They send him to Toyota school every few years to update and about fifteen years ago he became and maintains his master tech status.

If you have your heart set on a place you would kill to work at, you have nothing to lose (except the hourly wage) if you put something similar on your résumé's cover sheet, just as Rod did in the story above. Change the amount of time if two weeks seems a little too long. Just stipulate you'd like to keep the tips you earn during the shifts so there are no misunderstandings. If you prove to them what a great, reliable server you are, and what an asset to the team you'll be, you will get the job and more than likely get paid from day one anyways.

When you go in to apply for a job, you've got one time to make a good first impression. Apply your make-up, do your hair, put on some heels and dress super nice. When girls come into our bar to apply for a job, their résumé is thrown into the garbage if they dress like a slob or they have spelling mistakes on it. Be friendly, polite, and outgoing, remember your manners and smile!

When dropping off your résumé, don't go into restaurants and diners during lunch hours (usually after 11:00 am and before 2:00 pm) since this is when they have their lunch rush and staff is busy. If you want to apply at a pub, bar or strip club, go in when the business opens (or call to ask when the manager is in). If the boss is not in, ask when would be a good time to come by and drop off a résumé. Don't bother leaving your résumé with anyone there. Sometimes they aren't given to the person in charge anyways, are misplaced or even thrown into the garbage. You want the manager to meet with you and see what a great asset you would be to his team.

When asked about your serving experience, be honest! If you don't have any type of serving experience, you may have to apply anywhere and everywhere. You'll just have to see who's willing to give you a shot. If you end up getting a call from a dumpy diner, take the job. It doesn't mean you have to work there the rest of your life. Use it to gain some experience and once you feel confident in your serving abilities, try applying for the dream bar jobs again.

Do you know if your province's laws state that you must have a serving certificate in order to serve alcohol or even food to the public? In British Columbia it is law to have a "Serving it Right" card before anyone can serve alcohol in an establishment. To aid in your chances of getting hired for a job, look into getting a "Serving it Right" certificate if you want to serve alcohol before you even drop off your resume. Take the course and pass. Then put a photocopy of the card or certificate in your résumé. It doesn't take long and you do it online.

Congratulations! You Got the Job! Now you need to impress a lot of people: your new boss, your new coworkers and the customers.

Care of the Cocktail Waitress on the Inside and Out

Always do your Make-up and Hair

As you get comfortable at your job and the longer you stay, always stay in the habit of applying your makeup and doing your hair before going in for your shift. Over the years I've seen some coworkers get lazy and get into the bad habit of not putting on a stitch of make-up or doing their hair before coming to work and it looks unprofessional. Customers don't want to see what you look like on your day off, no matter what shift you're working, be it a busy Friday or a slow Tuesday. Put your make-up on, do your hair, shave and be conscious of your cleanliness and wear well put together clothing every single shift you work, no exceptions.

You're in an environment where you're constantly competing for attention against other servers, strippers (if you serve in a strip club) and "dolled up" female customers coming into the bar. You don't want to be known as the unkempt waiter or waitress. It's unsexy and you don't want guys thinking, "She reminds me of my wife with no make up on." Enough said….

Clothing

You're working in the serving industry, so pay special attention to your clothing. Obviously, you'll be told what the dress code is. Usually it's black skirt or pants, white or black top, black hose and shoes, unless you'll be given a uniform to wear. Don't show up to work with a dirty/stained or rumpled looking shirt or a baggy skirt two sizes too big for you. Never show up at work in jeans, no matter how nice they seem. There is nothing wrong with a nice, fitted, flattering low cut top showing great cleavage. Be proud of your looks. *Dress for Success.*

Treat Your Feet Like Gold

During the winter, black leggings with a skirt and flat heeled black boots are my comfort of choice. The leggings keep my legs warm and the boots look stylish and sexy. I wear socks in all my boots because the socks keep my feet toasty; they also soak up the sweat and keep my boots from stinking.

As the season starts to change and the weather warms up, keep cooler shoes ready to pull out at work. One day while you're at work, your feet will start to swell, hurt, and feel overheated. It will usually be when you're busy and running off your feet. That is the time for a change in footwear. Pulling off the boots, your calves will feel cooler and so will your feet. Pressure points will be changed and you feel like you can walk another ten miles with a change in footwear. If it wasn't for your feet, you wouldn't be able to work and make money, so treat them well!

If you're a woman who wears pantyhose, keep a couple extra pairs at work. It looks really tacky and unprofessional when a server has a big run or hole in them while she's working.

Years ago, we hired a server who would show up on a busy Friday afternoon in stripper shoes! She could barely walk and she struggled to keep balanced with her tray. I had mentioned to her that she should get some comfortable shoes or she will have no toes left at the end of the week. She mentioned they were just for fun. Not even an hour later she had changed her fun footwear to flip flops she had worn to work in the first place.

Nails

Nails are important as well. This is my weakness since I have horses I train during the summer. During the winter months when I spend less time with them, I put fake nails on. This is the time I'm showered with comments from guys on what beautiful nails I have. People see your hands when you set drinks down in front of them, give them change, shake their hand and collect empties. Unfortunately for me, horses and long nails don't go well together. During the summer months I keep my nails short and well manicured.

Other Important Ways to Take Care of Yourself

Rest

Your presentation isn't the only thing you need to keep on top of. Make sure you get a good night's sleep because rest is important. It keeps you awake and energized and your mental alertness is one hundred percent! Monitor the amount of time you spend in the socializing scene. After a shift, you can end up with your coworkers at someone's house for after-work cocktails. Before you know it, the sun is coming up. I know because I've been there! It's easy to get caught up in the bar life. You party all night and sleep all day. For some, it just doesn't work. We have personal obligations to fulfill and chores that need to be done. Perhaps you still have another day job as most friends of mine who work in the bar have. Some people (myself included) get headaches or migraines if they don't get their eight hours of sleep.

As you get to know the job, you'll know which days are your busiest and make you the most money. In the past, I worked Friday nights and my shift was nine hours long. It was the best shift of the week as I started early in the afternoon and served the guys getting off work and coming in with their buddies before the weekend. I made some great money because the crowd was older, full of blue collar workers and regulars were the main clientele during that time of the day. The shift switched gears to the dinner crowd and then the party room. I went home with stupid amounts of money in exchange for sore feet and shoulder/back aches. Often, I would dream of serving that night (the dreams were of me forgetting customer's orders or the bartender taking twenty minutes to get my drinks made for me ... all nightmares). I always made sure before my shift I didn't do anything too strenuous like doing loads of shopping or tons of errands. I basically hung out at home doing some light housework, reading or watch TV. I kept my day pretty mellow as I liked to save my energy for work on that long, busy, money-making night. I also made it a point to wear my most comfortable boots, tops and skirts. I made sure my hair wasn't falling into my eyes and I didn't have to keep sweeping it off my face, so it would be partially clipped back.

Eating

Eat before going to work so you're not concentrating on your stomach grumbling and wondering when you're able to go on a break to eat. Bars ARE the service industry and if the bar is busy and packed, you may not be allowed to go on a break during your scheduled time. You are there to serve and sell. I've worked nine hour shifts in the past without a break because that's how busy the bar was.

If you're diabetic or need to eat, be prepared to eat on the run. Ask your boss where you could keep something to eat that is convenient but out of the way and let him know of your diabetes. Use your best judgment and don't order messy food like a cheeseburger or steak.

If you're new, don't start making demands about eating and needing a break. Go with the flow and wait for the head waitress or boss to give you the okay to head off for your break.

Watch what you eat before a shift. I'll say one word and that is gas. If you're gassy, Tums help settle a tummy but there's not much you can do for the farts. One of my coworkers would feel the pressure build and run into a big group of people (always "the non-tippers," she explained) and release the pressure, then briskly walked away. Although it was very unprofessional, it was quite comical and she felt it was kind of a payback to the non-tippers.

Cell Phones

Cell phones are a big part of almost everyone's life. Keep your cell phone in your purse and don't bring it near the bar. It's distracting and you will not be able to concentrate on your job if you're answering calls or if you keep reading and sending text messages. If you're checking your cell at the bar, you'll end up standing in the way of other servers trying to get to the till and this is annoying to a server like me. I'm there to work and make money, not waste precious time on my cell phone. If the boss walks in and sees you on your cell, it doesn't look good. If customers see you on your phone while their drinks are empty, you might as well say good bye to any tips and you may even make them so mad they won't come back.

Same goes for the business line in the bar. Don't hand out your work number to friends. The only people who have my work number are my husband, my daughter and my parents. They know it is for emergency purposes only.

Tips to Become a Well-Rounded Cocktail Server

As you get comfortable at your bar and you're learning all the ins and outs of cocktail waitressing, you'll want to learn more about this job.

Study your bartenders and ask questions when neither of you are very busy. When customers order drinks like a Harvey Wallbanger or a B52 shooter and you don't know what they contain, ask your bartender. The more information you know the better, because it could speed things up at the bar. One day, you could end up working with a new bartender who might not know what a Dirty Hooker shooter is, but you will.

Years ago, I went to the Dollar Store and picked up a recipe card holder and recipe cards. I spent a slow Tuesday dayshift writing out all our cocktails and shooters we make in the bar. It is kept behind the bar and when a new person works and doesn't know a recipe, help is close at hand. It has become a life saver more times than I can remember and is still used to this day. Don't feel threatened and feel like you need to memorize a trillion drinks if you buy a bartending recipe book. Most people order common drinks like screwdrivers, long islands and beer anyways. When customers ask me, "Could you please bring me four pink caboose shooters?" I'll ask what is in them and the response is usually, "I don't know, but they make them at the Yippee Kiay Bar down the street." A lot of people don't know that bartenders make up their own drinks and shots and throw a name at them. So, unless you know what's in it, you may be out of luck. Take initiative and write out your bar's recipes if it might help your bar out.

Learning to bartend comes in handy. If your bartender leaps over the bar to help the doorman break up a fight, you'll be able to grab your own drinks or help out customers standing in the line. I have come into work a few times on my day shift and I had no bartender for the first hour of my shift. He didn't know he was on the schedule. I served and bartended by myself until help arrived.

Ask the bartender to show you how to change the keg and the boxes of syrup during slow times. Know where to get extra stock such as coffee filters, shot glasses, till tape, etc. Everything new you learn to do can help out a fellow coworker or a new person when they're busy and need help. It makes you more valuable as an employee.

Know what drinks to add your garnishes to. Lime or lemon twists will usually be added to drinks that contain alcohol such as rum, gin, vodka and even tequila. Corona bottles should have a lime twist popped into the mouth as well. Some customers will specifically let you know, "No twist" if they don't want it.

Being the low man on the totem pole (the new server), you may be required to fill in the "not so popular shifts." You'll have to be pretty flexible in taking what's available and needs filling in. This may mean weekends, late evenings or long weekends. Coworkers may need their shifts covered for concerts, holidays, or some short notice event, so offer to cover for them. This is a good way of winning their friendship and you may need a favour in return some day. As my dad says, "You scratch my back, and I'll scratch yours!" At my bar I waited around for four years to get full-time serving hours before someone quit. I was a food runner, a shooter girl and a beer barrel girl. I was a jack of all trades.

***I will tell you one very important tidbit … if a bar has a slow turnover of servers (meaning that some of the girls have been working there for a number of years), it's a good possibility it is a very good place to work at. The clientele, staff, and money must all be good! That is why I hung in there as long as I did to wait for full-time serving shifts and I'm glad I did.

Be Known for Your Excellent Service WHILE Playing the Game!

A sociable and friendly server who gets you a drink in record time … it couldn't get any better than that! How could you not be a customer's favourite?

I have talked to endless customers about what rates high on a customer's list of their favourite server; most say it's a server's personality. They feel at home when they are greeted by a cheerful person. They like to receive a smile and be asked how their day is going. Sure, they love a pretty girl to look at, but if the server doesn't enjoy people and it shows through their personality, they won't make much money and they won't last long in the business. This rings true for male servers as well.

I've been told over the years from many of my regulars, if I ever decide to leave the bar, they want to know because they would follow me to the new bar I work at. I couldn't ask for a nicer compliment! I sometimes wonder what they would do if I went to work in a non-strip bar environment.

I'm flattered when regulars ask which section I'm serving and they go to the trouble of cramming themselves at the only available table in my area too small for their party. They drag chairs over from around the room.

A previous manager from many years ago told me once while he was in another bar forty-five minutes away, my name came up within a group. They were talking about "the awesome service from Romana," they get when they come to my bar. I'll never forget that flattering remark.

I've even had owners and managers of other bars (one as far as an hour away) offer me a job at their establishment. I'm a firm believer in staying loyal to a company, unless I'm extremely unhappy there or not treated fairly. The grass is not always greener on the other side so don't get in the habit of jumping ship and moving from bar to bar. Every time you start at a new place of work, you start at the bottom of the ladder and must work your way up. **Seniority is KING in business.**

It's not IF you will get hit on while working in a club or strip bar, but WHEN. It's a fact and you can't get around it. So, if you want to make a lot of money in this industry, it helps if you play the game. Playing the game means you go along and flirt with the guys who hit on you, so they'll give you that tip. Your voice may raise an octave or two and you find yourself giggling over some really bad jokes that don't even make sense. If it makes the customer feel special, then what is the harm in that? Everyone has a different reason for being in the bar. I love my regulars who all know I'm married. We do some harmless flirting, a hug … and that's as far as it goes. My wedding ring is my security blanket. All I have to do is show some Romeo my left hand and he backs off.

If you get hit on all the time and told you're beautiful, you should feel flattered because guys find you attractive. If you get mad or your boyfriend has a problem with this, maybe you shouldn't be serving in a strip bar or a nightclub. Sex sells, especially in this business and that is why we make good money in tips. Isn't that the reason why we're there in the first place?

"Ro, how does Rod handle you working in a strip bar?"

This is a common question most people ask me quite often. On more than one occasion, I've had young shooter girls complain to me about how their boyfriends hate them working in this environment and what should they do about it. Not much, I'm afraid. Either keep fighting with him about it until he figures out you're there to make money and you're not going to pick up strange men, quit the job, or dump him.

Some girls have had the problem of their man coming to work and sitting there staring at them through the course of their shift. They have a hard time concentrating on their job because it makes them uneasy.

I'm married to a smart man who understands what it takes to make money in this business.

The Nevers…

Never tell customers your problems. Everyone has their own problems to deal with and customers want to have a good time and forget their own troubles.

Never argue with customers. If there's a problem, settle it. If it's something silly such as the regular saying the draft beer tastes off, replace it with another. It could be the end of a keg.

NEVER argue with a beer drinker! I've been told this piece of advice years ago by a senior server.

Never bad mouth staff. Don't agree with customers if they start telling you, "So and so is a really crappy waitress and needs to get fired." Instead, stick up for her because she may be having a bad day.

Never argue with a coworker in the bar. Take it to the staff room and iron out the problem. This is a fun place for customers to hang out and they don't want to see drama.

Never discuss memos or problems you have with the bar to customers. It is extremely unprofessional.

Never interrupt your bartender or another server if they're in the middle of talking.

Never pick and choose serving your customers. Years ago we had a server who would avoid certain tables or customers because the people were too rowdy, too creepy, had too many women, made her too nervous, so on and so forth. Serve everyone and give them a chance.

Never walk up to a table to take an order while eating. People don't want to see you with a mouthful of chicken wings. It is rude and unprofessional.

Never interrupt people at the bar. One of my coworkers will always ask, "May I speak?" It's a polite habit to have as I will be memorizing a large order of drinks and trying to punch them into the till in order and I can't have anyone talking to me for twenty seconds or more. If I don't respond, I'll hold my hand up or shake my head and she'll wait until I'm done.

The Always…

Always stay positive. Instead of complaining and saying, "It's so dead!" It sounds better and more positive if you say, "It's not as busy as we'd like it to be."

Always use your manners! Use "Please," "Thank you," "You're welcome." Use your manners whether you receive a tip or not.

Always say "Have a great weekend," "Enjoy the rest of your day," or "See you next week," when your customers leave for the day.

Always greet customers with a smile when you arrive at their table. Say something like, "Hi everyone! How's your night going? What can I get for you guys?" Say it with enthusiasm.

Always walk over to a table who is flagging you down, even if they're in another server's section. If the room is busy, take the order. Either their server is not paying attention to them or she's too busy.

Most important Always … Every single server is **always replaceable**. There is always another girl or guy standing behind you waiting to take your job!

Your Personal Conduct While Off Duty

My husband said my job (in a minor sort of way) is in the public eye. I notice it when I have customers comment to me, "I saw you on Sunday afternoon shopping in London Drugs. That must've been your daughter you were with, right?" Or, "How was your dinner at the Keg last weekend? I presume that was your husband who you were dining with." I feel like my outside life lacks a bit of privacy at times.

So, while you're going on with your daily life, conduct yourself in a mature manner. This reflects on your place of work and yourself. I'm not saying you have to wear make-up and be all dolled up when you're out shopping for groceries, but be aware of your actions. If you're out drinking at another club, I'm sure you'll hear all about it if you decide to enter the wet t-shirt contest, decide to pee out in the parking lot or end up puking all over the bar.

Important Safety Tips at Your Job

You're in the public eye and mingle with many different people when you serve. You listen to your customer's stories and feel like you know their wives or kids after hearing about them a lot. Sometimes you don't even know they're married because they have never mentioned a family and with the subtle ways they hit on you, you've always thought they were single; there is also no hint of a wedding ring on their finger.

The bar brings out all types of people, so you've got to be able to keep a lookout for the creepers and the stalkers.

Some Basic Safety "Don'ts"

- *Don't* get in the habit of telling too many people exactly where you live, especially customers. It's not safe.

- *Don't* get in the habit of telling customers you'll be out of town, especially if you've told them where you live.

- *Don't* get into the habit of taking off with customers and partying with them after work. If you're dying to get to know the hot guy in the group, get into your own vehicle and meet them at the destination, preferably another bar or somewhere where there are lots of people. Bring a friend if you can and don't go to a house.

- *Don't* hand out your phone number to people like it's no big deal. I'm not saying that every person who walks into the bar is trouble and out to get you, you just want to stay safe and have some degree of privacy.

- *Don't* break up fights. Alcohol and testosterone is a recipe for a fight. Working in the bar, you will witness many of these. Years ago, we had a tiny shooter girl who would jump in and try to break up fights. We would get mad at her for getting involved and try to talk the guys out of the argument, as she stood there in her bikini. Guys will not listen to reason. If they're furious, watch out because fists will fly and you will get bowled over in the process! If you notice a couple of guys or a group start yelling at each other or you sense trouble brewing, let the doorman or bartender know immediately. They'll have to diffuse the argument, hopefully before it blows up into a fist fight. If a fight breaks out, get out of the way and yell for the doorman, DJ and bartender. It'll take a few guys to drag these troublemakers outdoors. Do not leave the room and follow the group outside. There should always be a few staff members who stay indoors to keep an eye on the room and the tills. Keep serving your drinks and try to keep some sort of normalcy in the room. A fight always seems to make people nervous and you'll find it'll clear out most of the room anyways.

- *Don't* wear flip flops in the bar. You could end up with glass in your foot if a glass or bottle breaks. If a bottle or something else slips off your tray, it could land on your foot. Wear footwear which covers your heel and toes. This is a Worker's Compensation Regulation.

- *Don't* throw or smash empty bottles into beer cases. Pieces of glass could end up flying out and landing in your eye.

- *Don't* be too trusting and believe all business cards. Anyone can get a business card made up. While people like to network and build their business, be wary about getting involved with people who approach you with their business at your place of work. I've had guys handing out their cards to dancers and staff at my bar saying he's an agent that could get them modeling work or work in the porn industry.

I knew a guy years ago who had professional-looking business cards made up that said he was a Playboy scout. Of course he wasn't, but it was his way of getting together with many young, gullible girls. I couldn't believe all the screaming girls who came running after our limo one night, as he would crack the windows a bit and hand out the business cards.

Getting to your Car SAFELY and Driving Home

I'm lucky our parking lot is just outside our front doors and I'm fortunate I always seem to end up parking near them. Regardless, I am always careful when I walk out to my car. If I feel uneasy or something just isn't right, I return inside and ask a coworker to escort me to my car. It pays to be extra careful and always listen to your gut. You don't want to end up in a bad situation because you're in a rush to get home. If I have items I need to bring home in the evening, I make sure to put them all in one bag so I'm not juggling and struggling with a whole bunch of stuff while trying to make it out safely to my vehicle.

A small tool like a compact flashlight could be used to defend your life. The bright light shuts down the attacker's iris, giving him a blind spot, and this gives you a chance to get away if you were to flash it in the eyes quickly. Although tasers and flashlights may be helpful, they are also tangible items which must be carried and could fail to work if they short-circuit or if the batteries die. Having awareness, knowledge and a focused mind are most important as the goal is to get away, not fight. Give up any property like your purse or wallet since it's not worth your life.

If you work downtown and you have to get to your car after hours in a parkade or parking lot, ALWAYS have someone escort you. You want to keep yourself from becoming a target. Stay off deserted streets which have no traffic or people traveling on foot. If your car is quite a ways away, pay for a taxi to drive you there. It's a small price to pay for your safety.

If you have no choice but to walk to your vehicle, before you leave the building, change your clothing into something which doesn't attract attention to yourself and remove or hide costume jewellery. Hide the hot, tight skirt and cute shoes in a bag and put on track pants. Walk in sneakers as they are more comfortable and perfect for running if you need to. Slip on a big coat to hide your figure.

Don't wear your hair in a ponytail because an attacker would have a firm grip on your hair if he were to grab you from behind.

Better yet, put on a cap or hat. It's better to look like a bum than a hot bombshell.

Hold an individual key in your hand and have it ready to jab at anyone if they were to jump on you. If you carry a purse, strap it on you under your coat; out of sight, out of mind. If you must carry a bag, hold it in the hand opposite the street. Walk near the curb, away from doorways and shrubbery, unless there are vehicles parked along the road. Never assume all parked vehicles are empty.

If you suspect you may be followed, cross the street and do not duck into dark alleys or a building. You want to stay out in the open where you can be seen.

If you think a vehicle might be following you, turn in the opposite direction and continue walking. Get the license plate number and write it on the back of your hand or even on the sidewalk (a lipstick will work if you have no pen).

Walk with a purpose in your step and keep an eye out for anyone approaching you. If someone were walking towards you, look them in the eye and hold eye contact as they pass. You will look confident and powerful with this attitude and you are less likely to be messed with.

As you near your car, peek in the front and backseat to make sure nobody is crouched and hiding inside. Slip inside and immediately lock your doors.

If you find a van parked next to your car, enter your car through the passenger side. Serial killers pull women into their vans while their victim is getting into their car. Ted Bundy, the serial killer, was well educated and good looking. He played on the sympathies of unsuspecting women by walking with a limp and a cane and by asking his victims for help into his car.

Driving home is another thing to be aware of. Always be aware of anyone following you, whether you just finished a day or nightshift. Some people are mentally unstable as you will find from reading the various stories throughout my book. I have been lucky through all the years of working at the bar that I haven't encountered too many problems but I am aware of the possibilities every time I drive home.

Once someone knows where I live, I would be very uncomfortable for the safety and invasion of privacy for my family and myself.

If you drive home late at night, try to get into the habit of stopping to fill up on gas during daylight instead of late at night. Make sure your vehicle is in good working order by keeping up with regular oil changes and tune ups.

Keep your car in gear as you wait at red lights. Make sure all your doors are locked once you are inside. If you feel threatened, hit the horn and as soon as it is safe, drive away.

If you know you are being followed by someone in another vehicle, do not drive home. Write down the license plate number if you can and drive to the police station or an open business where there are people.

If you happen to get into an accident on your drive home late at night, do not get out of your car unless the area is lit up and other people are there! I've heard of stories where a vehicle "bumps" into another one, the victim jumps out to survey the damage to her car and she gets attacked. Stay in your vehicle with the doors locked and call the police. If your cell phone is dead, crack your window open and ask the other party to call the police. Rather be safe than sorry.

What to Do In Case of an Attack

In case of an attack, do everything in your power to get away and out of your attacker's grip. Scream, hit, kick and scratch like a cat. Don't back down and reason, cry, plead, or try to buy yourself out of a situation. Don't let yourself be pulled into a vehicle, into a building or around a building. Stay where others can see you and drop to the ground if you have to in order to keep him from hauling you away.

If the attacker says to you, "If you scream, I'll kill you," do the opposite and start screaming. You want to create chaos and ruin his plans. I put my daughter into a kid's safety course when she was very young. They taught the youngsters to scream the word "FIRE!" instead of "HELP!" I learned that people respond to the word *fire* more than the word *help* if anyone were to hear you.

Don't hesitate to use your elbows to defend yourself since they are the strongest bones in the body. Kick the attacker in the groin or knees, or go for his eyes with your fingers or a car key. You are fighting for your life and you have one chance to do it, so don't panic—aim and hit hard!

If you have a bag or purse in your hand, swing it with all your might and hit him as hard as you can. If your attacker were to choke you out or get your hands tied, it is unlikely you will make it out of this situation alive. If he asks for your wallet or purse, don't hand it to him. Throw it away from you and then run in the opposite direction. He'll be more interested in your purse or wallet than you.

If you get into your vehicle and find someone pointing a gun at your head, do NOT drive off if he asks you. Slam the gas pedal with your foot and smash the car into anything. Your airbag will protect you and as soon as the car comes to a stop, jump out and run. He will get the worst of it.

If the creep has a gun and doesn't have a hold on you, run in a zig-zag pattern.

Some Self Defence Moves

Although the following are moves that may help if an attacker gets hold of you, do yourself a big favour and invest the time and money to take a self defence course to learn the proper techniques from a professional. Practice of this kind is needed so you get your body used to how quickly it needs to react in an attack and with what amount of force. One day it may come in handy and could save your life.

- Clap/smack your hands against the attacker's ears hard and quickly! It can cause him enough pain to release you and give you a chance to run!

- Karate-chop him in the throat.

- Gouge his eyes with your fingers. This move can be done if the attacker surprises you from behind. Pull your arms up and over your head and behind you.

- If you're attacked from behind, spin around and strike with your fist into the pelvis (below the stomach and hip bone). If you hit hard enough, it can be fractured since it is a very vulnerable area.

- If you're attacked at close range, like a stairwell, pull the attacker closer to you so you can reach with your thumb, middle finger, and index finger and squeeze his throat (trachea). This can cause damage, so only do this move in the event of an emergency.

- Look into learning Krav-maga. This is a fighting style that can be picked up very fast. It teaches you to hit an attacker in vulnerable areas whether you are smaller in size than him or you are outnumbered.

- I've heard Bas Rutten, the MMA fighter, comment that if you find yourself in a bad situation where you've got a drunken person who tries swinging at you, bend over quickly and pull his legs out from under him. Alcohol dulls a person's senses where his thinking is slowed down and this will give you time to get away. A woman may have more trouble than a man with this move as she does have less strength.

A note about car alarms

You can ask to see if it is a possibility to have your car alarm programmed so when you press the button on your wireless remote once, it will unlock the driver's door only. Pressed twice, it will unlock all four. Rod informed me the newer Toyota vehicles have this feature (my truck has it and it's super handy to have), but some of the after-market alarms MAY have it as well. This is a great feature to have when you need to quickly and safely slip into your vehicle at any time of the day without anyone surprising you by hopping into any one of the other doors.

Some alarms have a "Panic" button on the wireless remote. Pressed once, it turns the car alarm on. It is another great feature to have if you want to bring attention upon yourself or your vehicle.

If someone were to jump on you by your car, the button is pressed and it startles your attacker and may give you or him a chance to flee. To turn the alarm off, press unlock.

Server Sign Language Signals

I love sign language at work. It saves my voice during a shift and I don't have to interrupt a group while someone is talking. If I know what a group is drinking, it keeps me from walking over to them, therefore I'm saving time.

Here are a few of my favourites that work great!

When walking by a table and you make eye contact with a customer …

"Another Round?"

Put your finger up and twirl it up in the air, raise your eyebrows and nod your head yes. This signifies, "Would you like another round of drinks at your table?"

Customer means **yes**- if they nod their head yes, or repeat the finger twirl.

Customer means **no**- if they shake their head no or hands wave almost like a windshield wiper move.

"More Drinks?"

Put two fingers up (three, four, or five), raise your eyebrows and nod your head yes. This signifies, "Would you like two (three, four, or five) more drinks?"

Customer means **yes**- if they nod their head yes or put up the number of fingers noting the number of drinks wanted.

Customer means **no**- if they shake their head no or hands wave almost like a windshield wiper move.

"Your Usual?"

If a regular customer walks in and sits down, I'll wave at him. He'll wave back as a response. At this point I will raise my eyebrows and hold one finger up. This signifies I will bring your usual.

Customer means **yes**- if he smiles and nods or puts one finger in the air.

Customer means **no**- if he waves you over to him (this is a time when I find that he would like a pop because he's on his way to a meeting, needs to drive, just had dental work or is on some medication).

If regulars happen to change their drink choice that day, sometimes they will meet me at the till or on the way to their seat as soon as they walk in.

"Pint Please"

If it's one guy and he wants a pint of beer, he'll usually signal this to me by putting his hand in a fist and hold it with the thumb side up, heel end of hand down (like he's holding a make believe pint of beer in his hand).

If it's one guy and he wants more than one pint, he'll signal as above and with the other hand, he'll hold up the number of fingers signifying the number of pints wanted. Perhaps he has a friend or two arriving at any moment.

"The Usual for Everyone?"

If it's a table full of regulars who just sat down, I'll say my "Hello" and I'll make eye contact with everyone and say, "The usual for everyone?" I have everybody's drink memorized and know what to bring without asking.

All customers mean **yes**- if they all smile and nod. Any customer wanting a change of drink will speak up and let me know.

"A Jug of Beer?"

If a group of guys sit down and want a jug of beer, one person will signal to me by looking like he's putting his hands on the top and bottom of an imaginary cylinder. Then he'll put the number of fingers up signifying the number of empty glasses and mouth the word "glasses."

Another way customers signal a jug is by pointing at the jug on the table next to them and one guy will put the number of fingers up signifying the number of empty glasses.

"Double it Up"

If someone is drinking a single cocktail and they want a double on their next round, they will hold their drink up, point to their drink or hold their finger up and mouth the word, "double."

"Thank You!"

When a customer is handing over money for drinks or a tip, I will mouth "Thank you," as long as we have eye contact so I can save my voice.

"Bring the Bill, Please!"

There are a few different ways a customer will signal to me for their bill. A few are as follows:

- The customer will take their hand and make a big check mark in the air (like when your teacher in grade school would mark your exams with a check or an X).

- The customer will hold one hand out flat and use the other hand to look like they're writing on the flat hand.

- The customer will take his thumb, index (pointing) finger and middle finger and rub them together in the air.

In response, don't just walk away. Make sure you nod and acknowledge them. They may have a taxi waiting for them outside or they're in a rush to leave.

"Good Bye!"

A smile and a wave, while mouthing "Thank you," is nice to do when your customers are leaving.

Learn to read lips. Customers may want to change their drink order from a single to a double, or a double to a single. They may not be able to yell loudly enough above the music for you to hear.

Romana Van Lissum

Chapter 2
Selling

Bar Lingo / Terminology

This is basic bar terminology used by almost everyone in the bar industry. Different bars may have other terms they use, so get to know your own bar's terminology. This makes life easier for all.

Drinks

Cocktail A liquor and juice mix e.g., Vodka cranberry or Screwdriver (Vodka orange juice)

Hi Ball Cheap liquor (usually off the gun) served with a soft drink or water e.g., Vodka water, Rum coke and Gin tonic

Keg The beer companies sell big, round, metal containers full of draft beer. Our kegs hold approximately 59 Litres

Mix The pops and juices available to add to a drink. They can be on the gun or out of a can or tetra pack

On the Gun Cheap (house) liquor on the gun. This is metered and pours a full ounce at the press of a button

Pint/Mug of beer A pint of beer poured out of the tap

Premium Liquor Higher end liquor poured out of the bottle (not put on the gun)

Sleeve A sleeve of beer poured out of the tap. It is slightly less than a pint

Tap Draft beer poured into a glass or mug once the handle is pulled to open it

Drink Ordering Terms

Bloody Caesar	A Caesar made with tomato juice, instead of the usual clamato juice
Clam Eye *Pint with Clam*	A pint of beer with clamato juice
Coke Back *Water Back*	The liquor is poured over ice and the mix will be put on the side in a separate glass. The customer adds the amount of mix depending on the strength he likes - e.g., "Vodka over, coke back" and "Rye over, water back"
Cubra Libra *Rum coke with a twist*	A rum coke with a twist of lime. I find the only people who use this term are men in their late sixties
Dark and dirty	A dark rum and coke
Double dark and dirty	A double dark rum and coke
Easy Ice	A drink with few ice cubes
Extra Ice	A drink loaded with ice cubes
Extra Old Stock *(Molson's Beer)*	Customers may ask for this brand by using the term 'High-Test' or 'Black Label'
Frosty	A mug/pint glass that is kept in the cooler to keep it cold and frosty. (A&W does the same thing to their mugs)
Lime Cordial	Lime juice off the gun that some people add to their beer
Neat *No Ice* *Hold the Ice*	A drink with no ice e.g., "Rum coke neat", "Rum coke, no ice" and "Rum coke. Hold the ice"

Drink Ordering Terms

On the Rocks / *over*	A liquor on ice, with no mix. This is a single shot, unless otherwise specified that the customer wants a double or triple shot - e.g., "Vodka on the rocks" or "Vodka over"
Press	A drink with a shot of water (the water dilutes the drink) - e.g., "Rye coke press"
Wine Spritzer	A glass of red wine poured into a beer glass with half 7-Up and half soda water. Some people prefer ice and others don't. This drink has a stronger, drier taste
Red Eye / *Pint with Tomato*	A pint of beer with tomato juice
Round	An additional same drink to everyone at the table - e.g., "We'll grab another round"
Set-Up / *Mug of Ice* / *With*	A mug of ice that is served alongside a cider or cooler. e.g., "Pear cider with a set-up", "Peach cider with a mug of ice" and "Apple cider with"
Shandy	A pint with half 7-Up or ginger ale and the rest is draft beer
Straight Up	A liquor poured in a short glass with no ice and no mix - e.g., "A double shot of Grey Goose vodka straight up"
With a Twist	A drink served with a piece of lime (sometimes lemon) - e.g., "Vodka water with a twist"

Other Bar Terminology

Barred	A person not allowed to enter and be served in the establishment. Usually due to causing trouble such as fighting, harassing staff, etc. - e.g., "John Doe is barred"
Blue Collar Workers	People who work with their hands - e.g., Tradesmen: Mechanics, Landscapers, Roofers, Construction Workers, Plumbers …
Cash and Carry	When a server collects money for drinks as soon as they're delivered to a table. The opposite of running tab
Change the Keg *Tap the Keg*	When the keg runs out and a full one needs to be connected
Chiseler	A person who hasn't left a tip for the server or Stiff bartender
Colors	A gang's name or emblem on a jacket, vest or t-shirt - e.g., Hells Angels
Cut Off	A person that is not to be served any longer, usually due to intoxication - e.g., "That guy is cut off"
DD	DD stands for 'designated driver'. This person is responsible for driving his group of friends home safely and consumes no alcohol
Float	Money borrowed from the bar to use as change given to your customers when you deliver their drinks. It's returned to the bartender once you've earned the money back during your shift
Gratuity	Also known as 'a Tip'

Other Bar Terminology

Gyno Stage	This stands for 'gynecology row'. It is Gyno Row… seating situated at the stage where the guys are close enough to talk to the dancer
Stiffed	Not receiving a tip from someone
Head-Hunting	Stealing employees from another establishment (your competition)
ID	It means 'identification'
Padding a Tab	Charging a customer for drinks on his tab he didn't order and the server pockets the money
Promo	Short for 'promotion'. It is a free drink given to a customer that the bar pays for - e.g., "Please promo a pint for Jim"
Regulars	These are the same customers you see every day. You recognize them and you know their names and/or what they drink
Skimming	An employee stealing money out of the till
Slammed	The bar becomes very busy, very quickly; high energy
Straw Test	Retrieve a straw and slip it into a drink. Cover one end with your finger and bring the straw to your lips with your finger still covering the end. Once you put the straw into your mouth, take your finger off the end and the liquid will fall into your mouth. Voila! An easy way to have a taste without putting your germs into a drink

Other Bar Terminology

Tab *Open a Tab* *Start a Tab* *Keep a Tab Running*	You keep track of all drinks ordered by a customer and give them a bill when they're ready to leave. They pay in one lump sum at the end instead of every time you drop a drink off. Opposite of cash and carry.
Waitress Apron	A black apron a server wears to store pens, visa and interac slips, big bills, etc. This is usually used if there are no waitress boxes available.
Waitress Box	A lockable box bolted under the counter and used by a server for dropping any extra money, big bills, or visa or interac slips for safe keeping. The box has the server's name on it and there's a slit to slip money inside.
Waitress Section	A section of tables a waitress is responsible for during her shift.
Waitress Station	The area around the bar where the servers' till and dishwasher is located.
White Collar Workers *Suits*	People who are businessmen - e.g., Lawyers, Doctors, Stockbrokers, Investors…

Sales Strategies

A sales strategy is to up-sell a drink. This means to make a bigger sale. Big sales look good to the boss and they could possibly mean a bigger tip for you. I will give you a few examples to help you learn the art of up- selling.

Examples of Up-Selling: Scenarios #1–3

#1 "Gin Tonic?"

Patron asks the server, "Could I please have a gin tonic?"
Server replies with, "Would you like Bombay?"
Bombay is premium liquor, therefore more expensive.
Patron will usually answer, "Sure."
Server finishes up with, "Should we double it?"

In my experience, I would say about half the time, the customer will say "Yes."

#2 "Glass of Beer?"

Patron asks the server, "Could I please have a glass of beer?"
Server replies with, "A pint is a better deal today at $5.75. A glass is $4.35."

In my experience, most of the time the patron will change his mind and go for the pint.

#3 "A Round of Shots?"

Patron says to the server, "It's my buddy's birthday and we'd like a round of shots. Any suggestions on a good shooter?"
Server says, "How about Jagerbombs?"

A Jagerbomb is a drop shot. It's a shot of Jagermeister and you drop it in a glass with about an inch of Red Bull (or another brand of energy drink).

Jagerbombs in our bar are a little over $2.00 more expensive than a regular shooter. It takes up a bit more room on your tray (shot of Jagermeister and a tall glass with the small amount of energy drink). The shooter glass is dropped into the tall glass.

Re-Selling Drinks

During the course of the night, you may have gotten busy and decided to start taking out extra beers just to keep up to the volume of customers entering the room. As drink orders are caught up, you may have ended up with a few open beers left unsold on your tray.

I like to swing around the room a few times and if I haven't sold them by this point, I'll give them to my bartender to put on ice for me because I don't want the beers to be warm when I sell them.

If I gave him three Budweiser bottles, I'll write a reminder for myself, UP 3 BUD. I don't want to forget because they were rung into the till under my number and if I don't sell them, I'll be out that money. As soon as I get an order for Budweiser bottles, I remind my bartender I have my beers on ice so I don't have to ring them in again.

How to Get Rid of Abandoned Drinks

Sometimes I'll get an order for a mixed drink and the customer disappears. I can either dump the drink (which I never do because then I'm out that money) or try and re-sell it. I'll ask the other servers if anyone in their section is drinking the drink I need to get rid of. If I'm lucky and they just happen to need that drink, they pay me the money for it and take it away.

If a server can't help me out, I'll walk through the bar and ask if anyone wants to buy a crown ginger (or whatever drink I'm trying to get rid of). If it looks like a lot of beer drinkers, I'll be asking the younger customers and all customers drinking mixed drinks.

Sometimes the bartender can help me out and pour it into a drink where a double is needed. This will only happen when a server orders it because he can't do this for a customer at his bar.

Lower the Price

I'll lower the price of the drink by a couple of dollars. It's better to get rid of the drink as quickly as you can because the longer you wait, the ice starts to melt and then you sell a watered down drink to someone who will complain they can't taste the alcohol in it.

Remove the Ice

If I'm still having a problem getting rid of the drink and there's still plenty of time left in my shift, I'll bring the drink back to the bar. My bartender will strain the ice out and he'll set it aside for the next time someone orders that drink. I write myself a reminder, UP C/R GING. The next time a customer orders a crown ginger, my bartender will fill it with fresh ice and add a shot of ginger ale into it to bubble it up again.

Last Call: Final Chance to Sell All Open Drinks

When it's close to closing time, I'll collect any drinks sitting on ice or set aside and try to re-sell them to customers again.

If the drink is normally $6.25, I'll make a deal just to get rid of it. I'll say, "Hey guys, anyone craving for a crown ginger? Someone just ordered it and left. Now I need to get rid of it. It normally goes for $6.25, but I'll give it to you for ONLY $5.00!" Some of the time, they'll give me the $5.00 and other times they'll still leave me a tip, so I'm still making back all my money plus a tip. I would rather lose out on a couple bucks than lose out the entire price of the drink.

If it is last call and you still have those pesky drinks on your tray that you still can't seem to sell, you still have a few options. You can either give them away to some good regulars who would appreciate it, drink them yourself after closing or dump them down the sink. I have always gotten rid of my drinks. If I ever had to give them away, I would give them to either good regulars or the table that has been tipping me like crazy. They will remember this and I will have secured a tip for next time.

A Little Secret to Making Extra Money

There are several little things you can do to earn an extra tip which you will read about in the coming chapters. However, there is something extra you can do that can make you extra money very quickly and with very little effort. Let me explain…

Many times, customers ask me if they can buy me a drink. I thank them and tell them how much I appreciate it. I also mention that since drinking on shift is illegal, I would have to drink it after my shift is done. Usually they're fine with that and then either give me cash for the drink or tell me to put it on their tab. Instead of drinking a real cocktail after work, I pocket the money instead. It's an easy way to make some extra money and I find that the customer will usually tip on my drink as well which is an added bonus!

Sometimes a customer may want you to hang out and chat with him after work and have your drink with him. If you do, have your bartender make you a highball glass full of your mix of choice. Then place your garnish in it with a straw so it looks like the real deal. If you tell him you're drinking vodka, he'll never know that the drink is a virgin because vodka is colorless and odourless anyways. Vodka can also be mixed with basically anything; coke, diet coke, 7up, gingerale, cranberry, energy drink, water, tonic water and soda water.

Don't be rude and order a double or the most expensive liquor in the bar. If you pull a move like that, that may be the last time he will buy you a drink. I have many regulars who will tell me to add a drink on their tab for myself to drink after work. I always pocket the money since I'm there to make as much of it in a shift as I can and I will also be driving home after work anyways.

I work in a strip bar and sometimes guys want to buy drinks for the strippers. Some of the girls don't drink so I let those girls know about the pretend drinks as I just mentioned above. You obviously have to have a chat with her at the bar where the customer doesn't hear your conversation about this. The customer never knows she's drinking a virgin cocktail and he's happy to buy her a drink. I'm happy because I make a tip on the drink and split the cost of the drink with the dancer. (He may buy her more than one drink so I keep track on a scrap piece of paper and I'll give her half the money when the customer leaves).

I recommend not getting too friendly and hanging out drinking with new guys you've never seen before. You don't want to give guys the wrong message and you want to be careful of the weirdos. It's best to just thank someone for the drink and tell them you'll drink it after work. If someone tells you that he'll only buy you a drink if you sit with him and drink with him after work, just smile and say "Thanks anyways," and walk away.

By pocketing the money instead of buying that after work cocktail, you'll be amazed at how quickly it'll add up by the end of the week!

Important Tips for Running Tabs

During the course of a shift, you may be asked to run tabs with several customers, so it's up to you as a server to pay for all drinks rung in during your shift to the bar. If someone were to leave on their bill, you will be responsible to pay for it.

The information I'm about to provide for you about tabs relates to working in a bar where it's easy for customers to move around or even leave, such as a nightclub or strip bar environment. The servers who work in pubs or restaurants will also find much of this information valuable where possible dine and dashes occur.

Why do Customers Prefer to Run a Tab?

- It's more convenient since they don't have to go through the hassle of pulling out their wallet every time you deliver a drink. They don't want their wallet sitting on the table in plain view either.

- They don't want to be bothered tipping you every single time you make a drink delivery. They would prefer to leave one tip at the end.

- They want good service, knowing you will be working your tail off to earn that tip.

Advantages of Running a Tabs

You could be asked by every type of person to run a tab, so be prepared for the nineteen-year-old to the little old man. It could be the scruffiest of the clientele to the clean-cut businessman in a suit. **NEVER** make assumptions on who will tip you. You may get an unexpected bigger tip from the youngest person and receive absolutely nothing from the businessman who wears the fancy suit and expensive gold watch.

Running tabs are great time savers. When a drink is ordered, you can drop it off without interrupting a customer while he's talking and it also saves you time from standing there waiting for him to dig out money.

Running tabs can save you from losing money. When a drink is ordered and you drop it off, a customer may need to use the ATM machine if they have no cash on them. Other times, you may have to go back to that table for money since the person who is supposed to pay is in the restroom or outside having a cigarette. When you're busy, you could forget to go back and collect your money, resulting in your ending up paying for that person's drink. Consider yourself lucky when a customer will be honest enough to remind you that he owes you money if you happen to forget.

Running tabs can make you a bigger tip. If the customer loves your service and personality, you may be left with an even more generous tip than if he were to pay for all his drinks separately.

Protect Yourself: Scenarios #1–8

There are several ways to make sure customers don't leave you with their bill. Below are some scenarios I use to make judgment calls on running tabs with customers. The longer you are a server, you will learn to trust your instinct and make your own individual decisions on running tabs.

Scenario #1

Jim and Bob come into the bar. They're regulars I have known for over eight years and I know them by name and what they drink. They always run a tab and pay me cash before they leave for the night. I see them in the bar once every two weeks.

I will not bother them and waste my time asking for a credit card since they have proved themselves in the past to be trustworthy by paying their tab before leaving.

Scenario #2

My Friday night crew of eight guys comes in and each guy runs a separate tab. I've known them for years. There's a new guy in the group I've never seen before today.

I will not bother the new guy for a credit card. Someone in the group obviously invited him along. If I'm unsure, I whisper to one of the guys asking who he came with.

Scenario #3

Larry, Sam, and David come in. I've had problems with them taking off on their tabs in the past.
If they're bad boys and tip extremely well, I run them a tab, but try to keep an eye on them in case they happen to leave. If they leave, they'll make it up to me with a big tip the next time they return.

*If they don't leave handsome tips, I tell them they have to leave me a credit card or some cash.
If they complain about it, I explain to them that I have to pay their bill when they leave and then have to wait for them to return to get my money owed to me. I also add it's an inconvenience to me as I have my own bills to pay.*

Scenario #4

Two young guys I don't recognize come in during the dayshift. They order a jug and ask me for food menus. They ask me if they can run a tab.

I'll ask them if they'll be leaving the room at the same time to go outside for a cigarette at some point.

If they say YES, I tell them I need a credit card and driver's license to run a tab.
If they say NO, I'll say, "One guy has to sit in the room at all times. If you both need to leave the room, you'll have to give me a credit card and driver's license to keep your tab open or you need to pay before you leave." This way they know I expect *one guy to stay in the room at all times.*

Scenario #5

A young guy I don't recognize comes in during the nightshift. He orders a pint of beer and wants to run a tab.

*I tell him I need a credit card and driver's license to run a tab. I know he'll need to leave the room at some point to use the restroom. Night shift can get hectic and I don't have time to keep an eye on customers.

Scenario #6

Two older, well-dressed guys come in during the dayshift. They just want to have a few drinks. I ask them if they will be leaving the room to have a cigarette at some point.

*If they say NO but leave the room anyways, leaving their cell phones and keys on the table, I don't panic. They will be back.

Scenario #7

A couple of guys come in during the dayshift, they order lunch and drinks. They say they're only having a couple rounds of drinks and they want to order food. They mention that they want to pay their bill by debit. One guy runs out of the room answering his cell phone as the other guy gets up a few minutes later to go outside for a cigarette. (There are no coats, keys, or cell phones at the table).

I stop the smoker and say, "Honey, could I please get a credit card before you leave the room? It's the bar's policy and I have been burned with a $130.00 tab someone had left me with in the past."
Explanation: Referring to him as HONEY is endearing. Guys love getting called Honey from a girl they don't know. If you explain it's the bar's policy, it puts the blame on the bar. The story about you being left with a $130.00 tab makes him feel sympathetic to your story (If you've never been left with a tab, LIE and tell people it's happened to you anyways).

Scenario #8

A stag comes into the bar and all the guys in the group want to pay separately with cash.

You tell the driver or the oldest and most responsible looking person, "Because it's a stag, it's the bar's policy that someone in the group must leave a credit card and driver's license at the bar. This way if there's any trouble or damage management can contact your party."
Explanation: The guy handing his credit card over will MAKE SURE everyone is well behaved and nothing will get damaged in the bar.

Other Important Rules to Running Tabs

There is still a couple ways to protect yourself if your customers are adamant about running tabs but they don't want to hand over their credit card and ID, they forgot it at home or they claim they don't own one.

1. If the customer hands over a bank card, DO NOT TAKE IT! It doesn't help you if they disappear. This is what happened

to me when I got left with that $130.00 tab I keep talking about. I even called the bank and the woman on the other end told me that all she could do was get a hold of the owner to let him know about the bill and then she asked me why I didn't grab a credit card in the first place. The guy probably laughs to this day and got another bank card.

If the customer hands you his bank card and driver's license, don't take it either. These don't pay the bill if they disappear and leave. I don't take car keys, wallets or promises to give me their first born. I want to see a credit card and driver's license or cold, hard cash. This is your money and you're there to make it, not buy other people drinks and work for free.

2. If the customer pulls out a stack of paper money to prove he has cash to pay his bill, I respond with, "Honey, I can run you a tab if you give me some cash to hang onto." I'm usually handed anywhere from $50.00 to $300.00, depending on the amount of drinking the customer and his friends plan on doing.

3. I point to where the ATM machine is so he can retrieve cash. If he doesn't want to get up right away because there's a naked girl on stage, I let him know I'll collect when her show is over (and I write myself a quick note that he owes me money so I don't forget).

Sometimes, people don't want to use those little ATM machines standing in the corner of a room. They don't trust the security of it, they don't want to pay the high fees and sometimes the machine is down and not working anyways. Customers are very appreciative of the fact I offer to swipe their debit card and help them take money out of the debit machine at the bar.

4. Customers ask me if they can get cash back with their credit card. We're not really supposed to do this because of the

credit card fees and for security reasons as the card could be stolen. I do it only if the customer is a regular because I will know him and I let him know I'm not supposed to be doing it in the first place, so he will not expect it every time he comes into the bar.

5. If someone you don't know hands you a credit card to run him a tab, it's a good idea to ask him for identification. If the name and signature match to the photo, that person should be the rightful owner.

   Some customers have commented to me, "Why should I trust you with my credit card and ID?"

   I'll respond with, "Why should I trust you not to leave on your tab? I've been working here for over twenty years and I have never lost a credit card. Besides, if you leave, I'm stuck paying your bill."

6. Many people have this misconception if a bill were left unpaid, the bar takes it over and pays for it. WRONG! The server is responsible for it. Not everyone is a scammer and leaves you with his bill on purpose. Some people have a little too much to drink and they don't even realize they haven't paid their tab. Patrons run outside for a quiet place to talk on their cell phone, converse a little longer than usual, and then autopilot kicks in as they head to their car and forget to pay their tab. Before you know it, you're stuck with their bill and would you recognize these people a few weeks or even months later? Servers see hundreds of people a week and it takes me a few times before someone looks remotely familiar.

7. If I'm working the nightshift and I don't recognize a person who wants to run a tab, I will definitely not run a tab without some sort of collateral. The nightshift crowd drinks a little more, parties harder and are mostly younger in age.

The dayshift crowd is a little quieter. A lot of guys will come in by themselves, as well as people who are on their lunch break. It's not unusual to see a guy working on his paperwork or a laptop. The energy in the room is a little more subdued and mellow. I still try to keep to my rules on running tabs as I've been left with a few of them in the past during the dayshift as well.

Every now and then on the dayshift, I break my own rule about asking a customer for their credit card. I think to myself, "That guy looks like a normal kind of person who won't bolt on his tab. He's by himself and he's eating lunch. He'll probably have a couple beers and then go." Before I know it, he's had six beers and I'm all jumpy because he's leaving to use the restroom. I hate being leery of people. It makes my job easier if I just have that credit card and ID as back up. If you find yourself gambling like this from time to time, you can still save yourself by mentioning to the customer that since their bill is around fifty dollars, they will either have to square up or give you a credit card and ID to continue running the tab. If they question this, blame it on the bar's policy (even if the bar doesn't have a policy like that. You're just trying to protect yourself).

8. Like I mentioned in a couple of the scenarios above, when I work the dayshift, I find that customers expect to automatically run a tab when they're ordering food from the kitchen. I always tell customers if they're planning on leaving the room to go have a cigarette or use the restroom, there always has to be one person sitting at the table at all times. If they all leave, they will either have to pay their bill or hand me a credit card and ID. If they ask me why, this is when I tell them about the stack of unpaid bills we have behind the bar.

9. When a customer hands you a credit card to run a tab, they may tell you they will be paying you cash at the end of the

night. Make a note of this at the top of the tab in case you forget or if another server ends up taking over the bill.

10. Customers appreciate it if you avoid any awkward moments. If it looks like a big group is going to run tabs, reply with, "Wow, this is a big group. Are all the tabs separate?"

11. Keep all credit cards in a safe place at the bar. Don't leave them sitting out in the open. People mingle around the bar and if there is a chance for a scammer to steal an unsecured card, it'll happen. Be aware and look after customers' credit cards as though they were your own. It would be extremely hard and embarrassing to explain to a customer who has put his trust in you to keep his card safe that his credit card was stolen and he has to put a hold on it or cancel it.

12. I've been told by a fellow server when she worked at another pub, at the end of every shift, all the servers put one dollar into the dine-and-dash kitty. This way, if a customer leaves on his bill, there's money in the kitty to pay the server, so she's not out that money. It's a great system for new servers, but I would never take advantage of it since I'm on top of all my tabs and I see it as my fault if a customer leaves when I didn't have some insurance (a credit card or cash) to run the tab.

I also feel it allows some servers to have a sense that it's okay not to stay on top of their tabs because the fund will always be there to save them. Some servers will take advantage of this system and everyone else will be left with nothing. I don't want to pay a dollar into a kitty when I know I will rarely need it. A dollar a shift times the amount of shifts per week; five shifts a week equals $5.00, in a month that is $20.00, in a year it would be $240.00! What if a customer comes back a day later and realizes he left on his tab the previous day? Would you trust the girl to put the money back she took out of the kitty the day before?

13. When a customer hands you a credit card, it's extremely important to do a quick inspection of it. Make sure there's no sticker on it reminding the customer to call in and validate it. If they didn't do this when getting the card, they won't be able to use it. Inspect the expiration date because if it's before today's date, it will be declined. Look at the front and back and make sure it hasn't been altered in some way. Also check that it doesn't have a woman's name on it since some guys carry their wife's credit card (I've had this happen a few times).

14. When you deliver a tab with the customer's credit card and ID, make sure he's sitting there before you drop it off. You don't want to leave it at his table when he's out having a smoke or in the restroom because the credit card can be stolen.

15. Do not accept Travelers Cheques. They are easy to alter and steal.

16. When a credit card says "preferred customer" on it, it means it's a pre-paid credit card and sometimes these cards rarely have a balance left on it. We make it policy in our bar that we do not accept these cards if a customer wants to run a tab or pay with it because there was a notice put out a few years ago that there was over $100 000.00 worth of these cards circulating that were stolen.

17. If another server's customer is in a rush to leave, I will help out if I'm not busy. I'll find the bill, run over to the server responsible for it and ask her if the tab is updated and explain they need to leave right away. She may ask me to run it through for her and other times she'll want to deal with it herself.

Tabs are a big part of serving, so ask your senior server any questions you may have about them. You will want to know all the bar's rules and any policies related to them.

Organizing and Reading Tabs

Sometimes there could be more than a dozen or so credit cards and tabs waiting by the till between all servers. There must be some sort of organization system to keep all these tabs from getting mixed up.

Every server should have her own glass that houses all her tabs. As I get a credit card, at the top of the bill I write the customer's first name and last four digits on the credit card, as well as the table they're sitting at in the room. The reason I use the first name is because it is more personal. If you feel more comfortable writing the person's last name, do that (this would be better to do because it would be more obvious to notice if you gave the wrong credit card back to a customer).

If your place of work doesn't have waitress boxes, ask your liquor reps to get you a waitress apron. They are great to hold all your credit cards, visa slips, pens, big bills, etc. Usually the liquor reps can get them for you for free. If that is not an option, look online and purchase one.

When you're preparing to sign off someone's tab, ALWAYS double check the name and digits so they match the name on the credit card and driver's license. There could be three tabs with the same first name on them. When I was still a rookie at this job, I mixed up a couple of credit cards. I was lucky they were both regulars so they were nice about it. I didn't know I had mixed them up until I came to work the next day and was told by the senior waitress at that time about it. I was mortified. She was able to straighten everything out because she also worked in the office. To this day, I am careful to double and triple check all tabs!

Securing a Tip

Every day a customer is faced with the decision of where to spend their money when they want to go out on the town and have a few drinks. There are many good establishments to go to and if a patron ends up walking into your place of work, you'll want to do everything in your power to make their visit as enjoyable as possible and you'll want them to return.

What is an Average Tip?

Many new servers who are starting in the industry may wonder what an average tip is. You must have an idea, as I'm sure many of you tip servers when you go out.

The average tip is between 10 and 20 percent. If you're not sure how to work out what 10 percent is, take the total amount of the bill and move the decimal point one spot to the left.

Examples:

$50.00 - 10% is $5.00

$50.00 - 15% is $7.50
(5% is half of $5.00= $2.50 plus the $5.00)

$50.00 - 20% is $10.00

The main reason we work in the hospitality industry is to make tips. **TIPS** stands for **To Insure Prompt Service**. It doesn't mean, "Because I ran up to the bar and grabbed a drink for you, you have to give me a tip." This is often forgotten by many in the serving industry.

If customers are not tipping, there is usually a reason for it.

1. The service is extremely slow. You're stopping to chat with people and taking forever to deliver their drinks.

2. You have forgotten their order or keep forgetting about them.

3. You're grumpy, rude or seem mad.

4. They don't believe in tipping (while they don't get tipped at their job, they feel we don't deserve to be tipped).

5. They don't know what a tip is (this is usually the younger generation).

6. They can't afford it or don't have extra money to leave you a tip.

Customers may want you to get things for them other than drinks and shooters. If you do the little extras, a tip may be rewarded.

• I've been asked to get customers a pack of cigarettes. When I get them, I remove the plastic wrapping and slip a pack of matches to the customer at the same time. They'll appreciate the thought.

• Customers have asked me to get bags of chips out of the vending machine for them.

• Redeeming keno slips and removing pull tabs out of the machine is another way to help out a patron and possibly receive a tip.

• Customers will ask me if I can give them money in exchange for winning pull tabs. I don't mind as long as they're not big winners I have to pay out more than twenty dollars. We had a problem with a $500 pull tab a few years ago. Each bar has a barcode on their winning pull tabs and in order to collect the money, the code must belong to the bar. If a customer redeems it at another establishment and gets paid out for it, the bar is out that money which will come back to the server or bartender who paid it out. You don't want to end up with a winning pull tab you paid someone out on and then find out it's from a bar located three hours away. You will owe the money back to the bar.

• I've been asked for Tums or aspirin by my regulars who have a hangover. I'll ask the person twenty minutes later how they're feeling and the response is usually, "Great! You're a lifesaver!" (I don't make it a habit of giving headache medication to an intoxicated patron as it's not good to mix with alcohol).

• If I'm extremely busy and don't have the time to stand in front of machines and pump in coins, I let customers know. "I'm sorry Honey. During a time I'm not so busy, I would be happy to get you pull tabs/cigarettes, but right now I need to stay on top of all my drink orders. If you'd like, I can give you change, so you don't have to go and stand in line at the bar for it." Some customers compensate me by throwing a loonie on my tray.

- Calling a cab for customers is another nice gesture to do. My bartender is kind enough to do this for me as he has better access to the phone. The taxi company will want to know the customer's name and whether they'll be waiting at their table or at the door.

- Mentioning the special of the day when customers sit down could earn you more of a tip because of the cheaper price.

- Birthday celebrations and stag parties are great to serve because they keep you busy and reward you with some awesome tips if you show them a good time.

- Don't be so quick to dump drinks down the drain if people happen to get up and leave. Usually customers let me know they're going outside for a smoke and are coming back; however, some people walk outside without saying a word, go to the restroom or end up talking on their cell phone. If twenty minutes or so goes by and they haven't returned, I'll take their drinks and set them near the glass washer on the ledge. I'll let another half an hour or so go by and then dump the drinks if they haven't returned by that point.

If you dump someone's drink out by mistake and they get very upset about it, do the right thing and buy them another. Customers will always remember this kind gesture and you're sure to secure any tip given to you from them in the future. If you argue back and respond with, "Well, I didn't know you were coming back," they may never want to order from you again. Say good bye to any tips that would have been given to you in the future.

- Over the years, we've heard about jerks dropping date rape drugs into girls' drinks. I have many guy customers worry about someone dropping something into their drink while they use the restroom or go outside for a cigarette, so they'll bring their drink over to my till because they want me to keep an eye on it for them. I pacify them by telling them I'll leave it right beside my water by the till. This way it shows the drink won't be tampered with if I'm satisfied with my own water sitting there.

- Customers go to a bar to have a good time or to get away from their own problems. I've had customers in the past that have had a parent or pet pass away and I'll give them a few minutes of my time to tell them how sorry I am and give them a hug. I will usually buy them a drink to do something extra nice for them too. Years later, a few of these people told me how much that hug or talk meant to them. Be sympathetic to your customers and show them how much you care. After all, you are in an industry that shows you like people. Daily life is happening around us and as people enter the bar, they long to get away from the pains of broken marriages, deaths of pets or loved ones, financial troubles and other difficult situations they deal with. Giving someone just a few minutes of your time while they complain about their boss laying them off, troubles with their kids or wife leaving them will mean the world to them.

- Every time I greet a customer, I always ask how their day is going. Once in a while, the response is, "Not good. I've had such a bad day at work today, it's not even funny." This is a time that I feel is important to ask my bartender if he could please promo me a beer. I love it when I can smile, drop off a beer, and say, "Here Jim, this one is on the house. Hopefully this will make your day a little better!" I walk away while my customer sits there beaming and yelling out a warm, "Thank you Ro!" If there's no room on the promo tab, I'll pay for it myself.

- When customers order food and they're outside having a smoke, I like to pop my head outside the door and let them know their food is ready so it doesn't get cold. I make an effort to do this especially if it's one guy in a big group who's ordered food because I've seen friends polish off the guy's plate before he has a chance to return to his table.

- One of my bartenders goes that extra mile and offers samples when customers ask him what the difference is between the dark and the white beer we have on tap. They're grateful for the nice gesture and as a result, I always hear the tinkle of change in his tip jar. He gained us a happy customer who will definitely return.

- I have lent my jumper cables a few times to customers in need. It's a bit of an inconvenience but if I'm not busy I run outside to retrieve them from my truck.

- Once in a while, a regular wants to order another beer and tells me he's short a couple dollars. I don't make a big deal out of it and tell him to get me next time. These are the customers who will hand me a ten dollar bill and tell me to keep the change, saying they owed me some money from a couple weeks ago.

- Desperate customers craving for a cigarette are more than grateful if I can hunt one down for them and in exchange throw me a buck or two. I take the money they gave me and give it to the staff member or customer who gave me the cigarette in the first place.

Years ago when there were a lot more people smoking, if I found a pack of cigarettes and nobody claimed them, I kept them in my waitress box and kept them for customers in need.

The "Art" of Handing Back Change

Always carry change on your tray. I know of servers who don't carry any nickels and they're asking for trouble.

When I returned to work from a vacation not too long ago, I had a few regulars complain to me about the servers who ripped them off. A couple people threatened to go to management because they weren't given their nickels and because of this, they told me they didn't tip that server a penny— these are people who always tip me a dollar or more!

Absurd I know, but most people don't like you to assume that you can keep any of their change, no matter how small of an amount. If the customer returns, he may not tip you at all because of that dumb little move you made about not returning some measly little change. Let the customer be in control of keeping what he wants. After all, it is his money and by not handing back that measly little nickel, it is actually considered stealing.

If you happen to run out of change and you need to run to the bar to exchange a big bill, do it as soon as you can. You don't want to forget and have someone accuse you of stealing, even if you are the most honest person alive.

When a customer hands you a bill and says, "Keep the change," this means the small coin and it doesn't mean all of it unless he waves the bill away as you try handing it over to him.

If a customer mumbles, "Keep blah blah blah," where you can't understand what he said, always say, "I'm sorry, I didn't hear you." There's been a time when someone mumbled and actually said "Keep six" and I thought he said "Keep nine." I'm embarrassed when he yells, "Hold on! You still owe me three dollars!" I get flustered and feel like a dolt because I'm sure he thinks I tried ripping him off on purpose.

When dropping off a drink order and the customer tells you to keep the change that ends up being a nickel, I like to pretend I didn't hear him and set the nickel down in front of him anyways. I've heard of waitresses setting the nickel down and saying, "That's okay. You probably need this more than I do." I don't recommend you do this as you'll easily upset your customer and you may have screwed yourself out of any future tips. I like to put the nickel down so he realizes that that was all it really was. Your customer may not have been paying attention, didn't register the amount in his mind, or didn't hear you properly above the music. Most times I'll find a couple of dollars on the table when he leaves. Don't always think patrons want to rip you off on purpose. They get sidetracked by the TVs, their cell phones, naked girls on the stage, shooter girls and their buddies chatting with them.

Sometimes patrons who enter the bar tell you they don't want anything. The rule of our bar is that everyone must buy at least one drink, whether it's alcoholic or non-alcoholic. I explain to them it's the bar's policy and since we don't charge cover, this is the way we pay the dancers. Usually people understand once I explain this rule. Remember to always be nice about it as they will be paying for their bottle of water or pop and you might still get a tip from them. The only exception to this rule is limo drivers for large parties such as stags or birthdays where I give him a free pop or coffee.

People who expect to sit at a table and not order anything because they have no money make me want to give them a little talking to. They have to understand that servers are there to make money for the bar and when those non-drinkers take up chairs in a prime location, this upsets the server who is working that section. Servers want the patrons who are spending their money and tipping like crazy to be sitting at those tables.

As you get to know customers and serve them on a regular basis, some will eventually say, "Ro, every time you bring me a beer from now on, always make it $7.00," or, "Ro, whenever you serve me my pint, always take a dollar for yourself." This is the only time you are allowed to help yourself to the money. The first few times, the customer will usually remind me, "Did you take your dollar?" Always remember your manners and thank them before moving on.

Being a goof can usually work in your favour. During the slow parts of the dayshift, as a dancer walks into the room in her costume ready for her next show, I yell out, "Hey everybody! My friend Sandy Tease is in the house! Yahoo!" I start to clap and everyone responds by joining me in the clapping while they whistle and yell, "Yay!" It brings a little pep and energy into the atmosphere and the customers know that a dancer will be on stage momentarily. The girls tell me that they love it when I do this as it makes them feel a little special.

Pause for the Change

Ok, say a guy buys a beer that costs $5.25. He hands me over a twenty dollar bill. I'll set the bill on my tray and proceed to count his coins first and either hand them or place them in front of him on the table. I would first give back the $4.75 in change. Now, I move to the bills which are locked in my fingers under my tray. As I move my hand to pull out a ten or two fives, I'll watch out of the corner of my eye what the customer's next move is (it's like playing poker!). Does he just sit there staring at the stage or keep conversing with his buddy? Give him a moment to put his hand on the coin and see if he throws some onto your tray. He's making no move now, but there's still a 50 percent chance for him to leave some change on the table when he leaves. Does he scoop up all the change and slip it straight into his pocket or does he slowly fondle it, perhaps counting out what he wants to hand back to you. If he's fondling the change, pause a minute and give the table a quick wipe or pick up empties to give him a chance to give you a tip. Sometimes the fondling means he's counting his change to make sure you didn't rip him off.

If a customer gives you a twenty dollar bill for a few drinks that total $14.75, give back the change in separate bills and coin. This way, he will be inclined to give you a dollar or two. If you handed over a five dollar bill and a quarter, most likely you'll only end up with that quarter back on your tray.

Use your judgment when handing back change. If someone hands you two twenty dollar bills when their total came to $27.00, don't make them mad by handing back all their change in loonies. No one wants the weight of thirteen loonies. Besides, you don't want to run out of loonies before you get back to the bar.

I've heard a story similar to this one a few times ... a customer will enter the bar and pull out a fifty or one-hundred dollar bill. They will take the bill, rip it in half, and give you one half of it, saying to you, "We are celebrating my mother's birthday tonight. If the service is excellent, I will hand you the other piece of the bill at the end of the evening when I pay the bill." If this happens to you, run your tush off for this group and remember to be friendly and outgoing!

"We'll Leave You a Big Tip on the Table When we Leave"

Every server I talk to cringes when they hear that sentence! In chiseler terms they're actually saying, "I acknowledge the fact that I haven't tipped you and I'm not wanting to. You'll just think I forgot and not hold it against me." If they really wanted to tip the server, they wouldn't make that comment and would tip them then and there instead of making a big deal out of it, or they would just leave the tip on the table when they left. In my experience, the percentage rate of people not leaving a tip on the table after they make that annoying statement is about 98 percent.

Give Away the Extras & Emphasize the Freebies

When I drop off a bill for a customer, I like to include any type of promoting material such as tickets for future events. As I drop it off I say, "Thank you guys! Have a great night! I'll see you next time! By the way, I slipped you a couple of complimentary tickets to the Jell-O Wrestling Competition we're having here next week." They'll thank you for the tickets and may even ask you for some extras for friends they'd like to bring by as well. This considerate gesture may earn you a bigger tip. If they were nice, fun, and/or good tippers, you'd be delighted to serve them again. Happy customers become repeat customers who may end up becoming regulars; regulars are your bread and butter in this business.

When customers run a tab, depending on how much money they're spending, I'll give them a complimentary coffee or pop if they order one. If they bought four beers and a lunch and finish up by ordering a coffee, I won't charge them for the coffee. It's important to put the coffee on the bill and put a zero or no charge beside it. This way, when they look over the check, they'll see that it has been counted but not charged. If it wasn't put on the bill, they'll think that you forgot or they may have forgotten about the freebie themselves. It's obvious that people love things given to them for free. If they aren't charged for something as measly as a coffee, you may end up with a bigger tip.

When there's a group of people out to have a good time, such as celebrating a friend's birthday, give the birthday boy or girl a free shooter or drink. Usually, someone in the group will let you know and say, "It's my friend's birthday today. Does he get a free birthday drink?" I'll respond with, "I'll see what I can do!" When I return and drop off the free shot, I'll say "Happy Birthday!" The buddies think that you pulled some strings and you get all the credit. This may result in you getting better tips from this group.

Tips to Help Put Extra Cash in Your Pocket:

Have Fun as you work the Floor. As I walk around the room, I like to joke around and have fun with my customers. When this happens, a sincere smile ends up on your face. If it's one thing that can grate on a server's nerves, it's a customer making the comment, "Why aren't you smiling?" It can come out of the blue while you're cruising through the bar in a good mood and not expecting it. Try not to get upset as most of us do. If you give someone a dirty look or you say something back like, "Why don't you give me something to smile about?" you might as well say "good bye" to any tips. People don't tip bitchy girls.

I respond with a smile and say, "Oh, I'm just busy and concentrating!" and move on before the guy has a chance to make another irritating remark and gets me even more annoyed.

Keep your bad day at home! If you look mad at the world, neglect to smile, throw drinks down on tables, don't greet your customers and stomp around, you might as well say good bye to most of your tips that shift. I'm serious! I have had days where I'm in a crabby mood and notice how money is quickly slipped back into customer's pockets. Why should anyone want to tip a sour puss? Don't get in the habit of coming like this to work. Word travels fast between customers that "So and so is a bitch every time we come to the bar." I've heard it from customers about past servers.

People come into the bar for a good time and they'll pay for it, so if you're in one of your bad moods, snap out of it quick. In your car on the way to work, listen to your favourite tunes. Do whatever it takes to get into your happy place. You're there to make money, so make good use of your time and make as much money as you can!

Working on Your Birthday is not considered a bad thing when you work in the bar. Let all staff know about it and mention it as often as you can to customers! When a coworker works on their birthday, I mention it every time I walk by that person. "Hey guys, it's Laura's birthday today!" I'll say as I point at the shooter girl. When I'm at the bar waiting for my bartender to get my drinks and he's tending to his customers, "Hey guys, it's John's birthday today!" The DJ gets into it on the microphone and it's nice if that person makes a little extra cash on their special day. Helping out your coworkers this way means they'll reciprocate when it's your big day. I find I make big money on my birthday because customers will put extra money on my tray and tell me to buy a drink after work. I'm asked why I work on my birthday and my response is, "It's not a big deal, it's just another day." I bet a server would make even better money if she responded with, "I can't afford to take the day off." Maybe I'll try that next year.

Smile a Lot And Make Your Customer Feel Important! I mention this a few times in the book and as you can tell, it's one of the most important aspects to this job. You want to learn this mantra and always be mindful of it…

Smile when you're happy,
Smile when you're sad,
Smile when you're tired and
Smile when you're mad.

Happiness is contagious and when you see someone smiling, you feel happy.

When customers ask how you're doing, your reply should be "Fantastic!" Don't reply with, "Actually, my day is crappy because …" Nobody wants to hear your moaning. Customers come in for a good time and don't care to hear about your problems because they have their own to deal with. People like to tip happy and positive servers.

Make your customers feel important. If your regular tells you he's taking his wife to the new trendy Italian restaurant downtown for their anniversary or going on a family trip to Mexico, remember to ask about the restaurant visit or vacation the next time you see him. Your regular will feel important that you cared to remember this little piece of information and it shows you pay attention to them.

It's a good idea to know the area around where you work. From time to time, out-of-town patrons will ask where a good nearby sushi restaurant, bank or even a drug store is located. I've had dancers ask me where to go to have their broken heels on their shoes repaired or where a nearby tanning salon is located.

When a customer asks me for a suggestion on what is good to order on the food menu, I tell him. I have even steered customers away from certain dishes in the past because of portion size or complaints.

If customers seem to be in a rush, I'll ask them, "Do you need to be out of here at a certain time?" Clues to a rushed patron are the questions he'll ask. Questions such as, "What is fast to make on the menu?" or "How busy is the kitchen?" Usually they're pressed for time, hungry or perhaps even diabetic and need to eat right away. Once I put their order into the kitchen, I let them know that I explained to the cook to get their meal out ASAP. They appreciate that you made them a priority in the kitchen and you may end up with a bigger tip because of this. I'll even ask them if they'd like to pay their bill before their food arrives, so they can run out the door and get on their way. Halfway through their meal, stop and ask if they'll need a take-out container for any leftovers. Do everything you can to serve them quickly and finish in their time frame.

The high-maintenance customer can be a bit of a pain at times, especially when you're busy. This is the person who almost demands extras from you. Recently I had a customer ask about the steak which was on special that day. He wanted to know what type of steak it was, how much fat was on it, if he can substitute a baked potato instead of the mashed potato and if he can get a big mug of water at exactly the same time his meal arrives. You just have to smile and deal with it. If you want a good tip, do everything you can to make him happy.

The complainer is someone you'll have to learn to love. This is the person who will complain about everything. The music is too loud, the fries are too salty, the air conditioning is too cold and the serving size is too small. Be there for the customer to deal with their complaint because you want them to have an enjoyable experience at your establishment. Happy customers = Tips.

Promotions, Celebrations and Special Events

It's always a good idea to "spy" and see what's going on at other bars. By collecting paper advertising from tables of other establishments, you're able to see what's going on in the business of your competition. This is not just a job for management to do, but staff to do as well. It's advantageous for the bar to get input from all staff because everyone wants to see the bar busy and benefit from it.

Years ago, a big group of us who worked together, rented limos. We went out to dinner and did a strip bar crawl. It was a fun night out, socializing together as we ran into dancers and customers we knew along the way. We were able to compare things from other strip bars we liked and disliked and promote ideas to our own bar.

Busy bar = Making money for the bar owner and tips for yourself

Busy bar = Your shift feels like it flies by

Busy bar = You have job security

Busy bar = Happy customers who like the busy energy in the room

Busy bar = Happy staff, happy management, happy owners

When you're out socializing at other bars or pubs, strike up a conversation with new people you meet and tell them where you work. Invite them to your bar and tell them you'll buy them a beer if they come out to visit you. It's a great way to win new customers. I like to rave about the food we serve in our kitchen. It's fantastic and I mention it frequently as to why new people should stop in and visit us if they've never been there before.

Stags and Birthdays

I love stags. The guys are out for a good time and they'll pay for it. Most of the time I'll make awesome tips, my sales are high and I have almost as much fun as the guys do.

Make it a policy to grab a credit card and ID from one person in the stag group. This way, the group will be better behaved, knowing the bar has contact with the group in case of any trouble such as fighting or breakage.

Ask a guy in the group to give you the name of the groom/birthday person and then let the DJ know. The DJ will shower attention on the poor sap by letting the room full of people know it's his birthday, "It's Dave's birthday! Dave, could you please stand up?!" Sometimes the guy gets dragged on stage and the guy's friends love any opportunity to embarrass their buddy.

I like to give the stag/birthday guy a free shooter. It costs next to nothing and it's a great way to win over the group. I don't charge him for pop, water, or coffee either since the rest of the group will be spending lots of money on drinks, shooters, food and private dances. If there's a limo driver or designated driver, free water, pop, or coffee will be given to him as well. If it wasn't for this responsible and wonderful person, I'd be using up my time babysitting the group and calling for taxis instead of serving and making money.

I let the dancers know who "the special guy" is, and they'll pay extra attention to him. He'll end up with a poster or some other kind of promo. Of course, I arrange it and I look like the hero which results in big tips!

Some of the time, the groom will be dressed up in a funny get up. I've seen everything from diapers to tacky wedding dresses.

Many guys are on a quest to have every female sign their posters, hats, or t-shirts. This is a reminder of their stag/birthday night and I'm always asked to join in and sign these mementoes. I'm flattered to be part of these memories and because of this, I keep a sharpie in my bag and write the same quote. It's dirty, it's funny and the guys love it. I thank my friend and awesome bartender, Craig, for making it up.

Guy's Name,
Hope you enjoyed the **Licker**,
Thanks for **Cumming**!
Your waitress, Romana xo

You can use this verse if you'd like or think of something on your own, but have something prepared beforehand since it keeps you from racking your brain for something to write when you're busy. When you have a spare moment, sign away!

If you joke around, flirt, and have a good time with the group, you'll have loads of fun yourself, your shift will fly by and you'll walk away from your shift with lots of tips. You know you've shown a group a good time when you're tipped handsomely all night and as they leave, they come over to you at the till and gush about the great time they've had. They thank you for the great service and slip you another twenty dollar bill as they shake your hand, pat you on the back or even hug you. Don't forget, happy customers mean future customers. They are sure to come back, as well as tell all their friends how they had the time of their lives at your bar!

Don't be surprised if random guys walk into your bar and ask, "Are you Romana? Our buddy John was here a few months ago on Larry's stag and he said they had a great time that night. He wanted us to say hi to you." Even if I don't remember the person, I'll play dumb by responding with, "Oh, I remember John! What a great group of guys. Please say hi back to him for me!" This makes a positive impact on the new guys who came in. If they're new, nice, and tip well, treat them like gold. You want them to tell more friends and return.

Chapter 3
Organization in the Cocktail Waitress's World

The Cocktail Waitress Tool Kit

While you're at your job, take it seriously, have your tools, and *BE PREPARED!* I'm annoyed at coworkers who come to work forgetting their pens, calculators, aspirin, or tampons and think it's not a big deal. They think someone is always there to save them and lend them tools they didn't bother to remember to bring to work. Please don't be one of these annoying coworkers and always bring your tools to work.

I like to have a "work" emergency kit at all times. I like to refer to it more as a tool box or a tool kit. Mishaps can happen and if you live quite a distance away, hopping in your car to make a quick jaunt home is not always an option. I've had soles on boots rip open, skirts' zippers break and migraine headaches, to name a few inconveniences.

If you don't want to lug a bag back and forth from home to work, ask if there's a locker that can be used or at least leave it in your car. I like to keep my stuff locked away, as coworkers aren't afraid to help themselves to "borrow" something. Before you know it, your gum is gone, your tape has been used up and your pens have all disappeared.

I'll give you a list of items, which have become extremely useful to me over the years.

Clothing and Footwear:

Footwear

In a corner on the floor in the staff room, I keep an extra pair of shoes and boots. Zippers on boots can break and soles can fall apart. If your shift is long, a change of footwear is refreshing as pressure points will be relieved and you're able to finish off the rest of your shift in comfort. I keep a couple extra pairs of socks in my locker in case I arrive at work in flip flops.

I like to treat my feet and invest in some good insoles; the gel style is my favourite. I refer to the comfort of my boots as most valuable, so I don't skimp on paying good money for a costly pair to wear at work. I make a living working on my feet, so I like to treat them better than good. If I'm in pain, uncomfortable, or I can't walk, I won't be able to work and make money.

Skirts and Pants

I always keep one spare clean skirt in my locker at work. You never know when it could come in handy.

Tops and Blouses

My locker also contains a black tank top. Accidents such as spills can happen. At the first bar I worked at, I had a drunken girl throw her hands up in the air and she knocked my entire tray of shooters onto me and a customer. Back then, I had no spare clothing. Try explaining this story all night long when customers ask you what happened. The story got tiring to explain and it was pretty uncomfortable wandering around in sticky, stained clothing for the rest of my shift.

Some Basic Locker Necessities:

Shoe Polish

I have a baggie containing shoe polish for my boots. It keeps them shiny and moisturizes the leather so it keeps the boots looking new. You'd be amazed at how many guys have made comments about how nice my boots look. Yes, they look down, even in the dark.

Energy Drink

I have a couple of bottles of 5 hour Energy, which is an energy drink. For times I can't seem to stop yawning and need an extra boost of energy, I down a bottle of this stuff because I don't drink coffee and too much pop is hard on my stomach.

THE BAG and its Essentials:

I was wandering around Wal-Mart and found a cheap $7.00 men's shaving bag. It's not very attractive so someone will not be tempted to run off with it. I lock it up in my locker at the end of my shift before I go home.

It contains:

Gum

Gum is great to keep your breath fresh. Be aware of your breath after you eat especially garlic or spicy foods. If you have a cold, this is another reason you should be aware of stinky breath.

Note: If you're the type of person who chews gum like a cow, stay away from the gum and pop mints instead. Nothing looks more unattractive than a server smacking her gum like a truck driver!

Nail File and Nail Clippers

A snagged nail hurts like hell and drives a person crazy. I've even saved the day for a few bartenders by lending them this tool.

Nail Glue

If you have fake nails, do yourself a big favour and keep nail glue on hand since it will come in handy quite frequently for yourself and coworkers. In the past I've been caught without it and I hate feeling self conscious of my hand when I'm setting a drink down on a table or handing over change while a nail is missing. It looks so tacky and I can't wait to get home so I can glue the thing back on!

Keep a few spare nails on hand too, in case one pops off and you can't find it on the floor.

Mini Flashlight

I got one of these at the Dollar store for $1.00 ... big spender! I've had coins bounce to the floor and the flashlight helps me find them quickly. The flashlight has been used to scan the floor for missing wallets and cell phones. Customers with bad eye sight will borrow it to look at a food menu in the dark.

Pen Light

Do yourself a favour and purchase a pen light. They are hard to find and I found it at a hardware store for a few dollars and bought six of them. It is a pen that has a flashlight at the end. It has come in handy for looking at identification or money in the bar where the lighting is quite dark.

Roll of Tape

When bills rip apart, you want to marry the two pieces back together before you lose either one. "Out of Order" signs have needed to be put up on our vending machine, cigarette machine and bathroom stalls. "Kick me" signs can be taped to someone's back ... just kidding!

Pens

I have six at all times ... yes, six. One gets lost, someone borrows one, another runs out of ink. I always keep at least one clipped on the inside of my skirt beside my hip. This is my main tool to keep on hand.

Calculator

A calculator is used to add up bills, add credit card totals, do your cash-out at the end of your shift and work out tips split between servers. I have a small one with a cover on it that can be closed up when not in use, so others can't spill booze on it and get it ruined. I keep mine hidden until I need it and have 'Romana's – DON'T

TOUCH!' taped to the front. In the past, others would use my calculator and then leave it in the open to get sticky shooters spilled over it or leave it sitting in spilled alcohol on the counter.

Mini Stapler

When our main stapler at the bar disappears or jams up, and we're slamming busy, the last thing I have time for is to start pulling it apart and turn into the stapler-mechanic. The stapler is usually used to staple together Keno slips and our guest cheques. It has also been used in an emergency to staple ripped bills back together when the tape has mysteriously disappeared. You can even staple a hem back onto a skirt when you're in a rush as this holds until you have a chance to get it repaired.

Mini Kleenex Pack

This is great to have on hand for blowing your nose or blotting your lipstick when you don't have time to run to the restroom.

Mini Mirror

Having a tiny mirror nearby saves you time from running off to the bathroom when you need to re-apply lipstick or doing a quick check for boogers after blowing your nose.

Sharpie (felt marker)

This is handy to have on hand for writing out reservation signs and I've used it to sign hats and t-shirts for grooms on their stag nights. I lend it out to dancers needing to sign a poster for a customer.

"SHOUT" Individual Wipes

These are great to take out spots and stains. If you don't have these on hand, soda water with a clean rag works well too.

Hand Cream

I keep a small container of hand cream to cream hands and legs.

Tums

Great thing to have on hand for gas and tummy upsets. I've been the hero and saved the day for staff, dancers and customers when they ask me for Tums or aspirin; I don't give headache medication out to intoxicated patrons.

Aspirin

Used for relieving pain of headaches and menstrual cramps.

Lipstick or Lip Gloss

Keep nearby for those quick touch ups.

Crystal Light Packages

One of the girls at work got me hooked onto these, which slip easily into a purse and are great for flavouring a bottle of water.

Scissors

This is a very valuable tool useful for cutting up paper, reservation signs, loose threads, tags, etc. When they're not around, that's when you seem to need them the most.

Sample Bottle of Perfume

A quick freshen up.

Safety Pins

These are always handy to use for pinning bra straps or loose hems. I seem to get customers and dancers ask me for this little item quite regularly.

Travel Size Sewing Kit

During break time or after a shift, you can hand-sew a loose hem or button back on. This saves me from dragging it home during the week when it's not time to launder it yet. If I would take it home, the item would sit for a month in my way and I'd never repair it anyways.

Tampons and Pads

I'm sure you can figure it out.

Pit Stick

Convenient to have on hand for a mini freshen up. ONE DAY you might get to work on the busiest night of the week and you realized you forgot to apply your pit stick. It's happened to almost all of us.

Bandages

Keep a few of these on the side as the bar's stash can be used up quickly.

Small Antibacterial Lotion

I like to keep this beside the till and clean my hands periodically. Not too long ago, I bought a larger bottle with a pump which now sits on our staff table where we eat.

Hair Elastics and Hair Clip

I like to keep a few hair elastics and a hair clip on hand. During really hot weather where you feel like you'll die of heat exhaustion if you don't get your hair up off your neck, this is a life saver! It's handy to have around when I need a massage from the massage girl and need to pin my hair up and out of the way.

- The bag is great for keeping together any promoting cards or tickets you need to give away or sell.

Hang Onto Coworkers Phone Numbers

At home and in your cell phone, keep a list of all staff phone numbers. If you're sick or an emergency comes up, you can phone your manager to call in a replacement for you. If you can't get a hold of your manager, take initiative and call a replacement yourself. This way you can call your manager back and leave him a message saying that because he didn't answer his phone and you wanted to make sure your shift was covered, you got a hold of Lynne and she'll be covering your shift today because you're sick.

It's a good idea to keep all staff phone numbers. Keep numbers of servers, bartenders, DJs, kitchen staff, doormen and all management. You just never know who you need to contact, or you may be asked by a fellow coworker for someone's number. Never give out your coworkers' phone numbers out to customers.

The Ways You Can Protect Yourself From Losing Money

The reason why you're working in the first place is to make money, so keeping it safe and not losing any of it can be a challenge at times.

You look forward to doing your cash-out since you were busy all night and the majority of your customers were being more than generous with the tips. As the end of your shift nears, you do your last call, finish your clean up and lock up behind the last customer. You just want to grab your tip money and go home.

Unlocking your waitress box, you pull out all cash, credit card and interac slips, grab a cash-out sheet and start your calculations. Counting up what you owe as a tip for your bartender, DJ, doorman, and kitchen, it's set aside. Adding up all your interac and credit card slips, you subtract this total from your sales … that can't be right, thirty dollars? You re-calculate everything again and that's what you're left with. You killed yourself tonight for thirty bucks? You feel like crying! What happened?

At some point, every server has had a sinking feeling of lost money. It's happened to us all and it's one of the worst feelings in the world. I'm going to give you some tips on how to keep yourself from losing that precious money you've worked so hard to make.

Ask for a Credit Card AND Driver's License to Run a Tab

As I've already mentioned, I will always ask a patron I don't know for their credit card and driver's license if they want to run a tab. People get drunk, leave the room to answer their phone, use the restroom, go outside for a cigarette and then get sidetracked by forgetting about their bill and leaving. I see many faces every day and I wouldn't recognize some people the next time they returned anyways. I've been stuck once with a big bill for $130.00 and cried when I got home. It's bad enough when regulars take off without paying their bill, but a complete stranger who I would never recognize again, no thanks! I don't need the unnecessary headache of eyeballing strangers and with the credit card and driver's license in my hand, I can lower my stress level.

I don't ask regulars for a credit card if they have a proven track record, but the ones who are known for leaving without paying their tab, I won't start them one unless I have their card in my possession. For the regular who happens to leave on his bill, I let all servers know about it and leave a note by the till for the other girls because he may come in while another server is on shift. On the tab I write my name, the date, and then staple the bill behind the note. If the customer comes in while another girl is working, she'll collect the money for me, staple the cash to the bill and drop it in my box.

Don't let any customers bully you into running them a tab without some sort of collateral. It's completely up to the server to call the shots and while it is convenient for the server and patron, it's definitely not mandatory.

Having customers leave you with their unpaid tabs is one way of losing money, especially strangers you will never recognize again.

Claim All Credit Card and Interac Slips

While helping a customer retrieve money on their interac card at the debit machine by your till, don't walk away while the transaction is in motion and resist the urge to hand over any cash or let the customer leave until you see *Approved* on the final slip. See that slip in your mind's eye as cold hard cash. Don't leave your slips in a glass by the till or out in the open where someone could grab them or mistakenly throw them out. Store them in your waitress box for safe keeping. You don't want someone running off with an important piece of paper as a visa or interac slip. Every now and then, customers help themselves to random pieces of paper around my till so they could jot down a phone number.

Keep On Top of All Tabs

I know of a few bars that still run with an old till system, and to run tabs, you need to handwrite all drinks and food on a guest check. Our bar's till can let you keep track of tabs in it, but you can't have more than one server add to a tab, table numbers can't be changed if a customer moves, food can't be included, drinks can't be voided off and the tab can't be separated if customers need you to. There are too many steps to take in that bringing up a bill on the screen is just too confusing and time consuming. During busy times when three or more servers are working the till at the same time, it's just not practical to use so we all end up handwriting all bills anyways because it's just easier and quicker.

If your bar has a modern till system, consider yourself lucky that you can keep track of all customers' drinks on it. Make it a mission to learn the till and be quick about it as the newer systems are very user friendly and easy to operate.

If you handwrite your tabs and you feel as though you'll forget to write drinks down, do yourself a favour and ask your customers to pay you every time you bring them a drink in cash. If you explain you're new and still training, customers are pretty understanding.

I like tabs because it saves me time and saving time means I can use that time to make more money. I can drop off a round of drinks and not have to stop and wait for the group to stop talking or pull out their wallets and if a big group orders and they like to pay individually, this takes up even more of my valuable time.

When a new group sits down and asks you to run them a tab, find out if they're all on the same bill or separate. You don't want to try and separate four different tabs while you're busy and hold up other servers at the waitress station. When you start reorganizing bills and end up rushing, you get flustered and make mistakes, which could cost you money. Other customers will be waiting longer than necessary for their drinks and as a result you get confused and forgetful. Save yourself the time and aggravation by asking if all bills are kept separate in the first place.

I find that forgetting to write drinks or food on tabs is the number one money loser! Stay on top of your tabs or just do cash and carry.

Guard All Big Bills

When you're given a $50 or $100 bill, inspect it carefully to make sure it's real, then immediately stash it away. While working, don't fold big bills and slide them in between your fingers with your other bills as I once did because it was almost given away for change as a five dollar bill. I've known of girls stuffing their big bills into their boot or bra to keep from losing it and immediately dropping it into their box as soon as they get to the till.

Never leave loose bills lying on your tray because as you start to walk or air conditioning in the room blows at you, while you're looking in another direction, the bill may fly to the floor. I had a guy waving a five dollar bill while he chased me across the room once because he said it flew off my tray. I like to slip my bills into the side of the ashtrays stacked on my tray, place an empty bottle on them or clamp the loose bills in my fingers under my tray. If you feel uncomfortable doing either of these methods, set the bills on your tray and stack empties on top (never garbage). The bills may get wet from spillage on the tray, but you can always cram them in your waitress box while wet and by the end of the night they'll be dry. A wet bill is better than a lost bill. The reason you don't want to set garbage on top of any bills is because you'll scoop all the garbage and throw it into the trash can without realizing there may be money hidden underneath. I witnessed a waitress do this many years ago.

Big bills handed to a customer as change without realizing and money dropped onto the floor is a couple different ways of losing money.

Other Random Ways of Losing Money

• During a shift, you may have started taking extra drinks out on your tray when the bar starts to get busy or sometimes a customer orders a drink and then disappears. You'll try to sell these drinks to other people and if you can't seem to get rid of them, you take them back to the bar and give them back to the bartender. He'll put the opened bottles on ice to keep them cold and any mixed drinks will have the ice strained out to keep them from getting watered down. Make sure to write yourself a reminder of the drinks that were put behind the bar because you'll be paying the bar for these drinks if you don't resell them during your shift. As an example, if I gave the bartender five Coors Lights, I'll write myself a note reading, UP 5 COORS and keep the note in a glass by the till. As my shift progresses, I may need these drinks, so I reclaim them from the bar, deliver them to my customers and collect my money. If other servers order these drinks, the bartender will give them the opened beers and they can either pay me for the drinks or not ring them in or if they do ring them in, I'll void them later. This way, they're all sold by the end of the night and all I have to do is void them at the end of my shift if I need to.

Relying on your memory to re-sell drinks or not voiding the ones coworkers sold for you are other ways of losing money, so keep organized and jot down your random reminders.

• Another way a server can lose money is by not paying attention to how she's ringing drinks into the till and the bartender not catching the mistake. Let's say Budweiser bottles are on sale today at $5.35 and you must ring it in the till under the special beer of the day button (this depends on your till system). So, as you punch your order into the till, out of habit you're ringing the Budweiser beers under the regular button price of $5.75. You proceed to your customers and ask for the special price of $5.35. If they tip you $.25, you're still out 15 cents. Doing this periodically throughout a shift, you're ripping yourself off way too much money, so pay attention to how you're ringing drinks into the till, especially the daily specials!

Pay attention to how you ring in all your drinks, especially the specials of the day.

• Remember to get paid out on any tab from the server taking over if you're changing sections, the customer moves tables or you go off shift. I like to write the table number, the amount of the tab owed to me and which server took it over. I'll either throw the note into my waitress box or keep a running list of all tabs taken over on a scrap sheet of paper in a glass. This way, if I forget to collect on any tabs during my shift, I have a reminder in my box when I do my cash at the end of my shift.

Don't forget to get paid out from fellow coworkers on any tabs and tips owed to you.

• Be careful and slow when sliding bills out from between your fingers while your hand is underneath your tray.

If you pull too quickly, you may remove more than one bill and not realize as it falls to the floor.

• Have a system and keep all tabs with credit cards organized. You don't want to juggle separate slips, credit cards and bills and then give a customer the wrong bill or slip or even another person's credit card. How would you explain to a customer that you gave his credit card to a stranger and charged him for someone else's bill?

Mixing up tabs is a good way of losing money because the customer could get so mad they will refuse to pay the bill and leave.

• Another example of mixing up tabs is if you charged the first party at table #6 for two jugs and then they leave after signing off their bill. A short time later, the other tab at table

#33 informs you they ordered two jugs and not five you just charged them for.

If the first party wasn't honest and had quickly paid you for the two jugs and then left, you'll be stuck paying for the three remaining jugs you obviously can't charge the wrong party for.

Another way of mixing up tabs is another way of losing money.

- Do not accept old bills. Apologize and say that this is bar policy or you've had trouble with them in the past.

Accepting old bills that are fakes can lose you money.

- Do not accept bills from out of the country if you don't know how to inspect them for a counterfeit. I don't mind smaller American money, but I do not accept the $50 or $100 anymore as I do not deal with them very often and I'm not experienced in identifying the fakes anyways.

Accepting bills from out of the country that end up being counterfeit can lose you money.

- If your bar has a pull tab machine, be aware of what's in it and don't pay out large sums of money to big winners. Let the customer go up to the bartender to collect his money. All winning pull tabs must be redeemed at the bar that they are won at, as each bar's pull tabs have a code on them and if you pay out on a pull tab that didn't come out of your machine, you'll be responsible for paying it back to the bar. What if that pull tab came from five hours away? The only time I'll take any pull tabs is if a customer throws them on my tray as a tip.

Giving a customer money for pull tabs that weren't purchased at your bar is another way of losing money.

- Our bar is busy most of the time, so to keep myself organized when staff or dancers order food or drinks from me, I start a sheet of paper with their names and amounts owing. I like to start collecting on any outstanding bills from staff and dancers when I'm not busy or close to the end of my shift.

Forgetting to collect any money owing to you on food or drinks from staff or dancers is another way to lose money.

- During the nightshift, ask customers to pre-pay for all kitchen orders. The easiest time to do this is when you drop off cutlery, napkins and drinks before the food arrives.

It's too easy for someone to wolf down their food and run out the door without paying while you're busy and not paying attention.

- Pay attention to all change you're handing back to a customer. When a customer hands you a ten, place it on top of your tray and hand back the change, counting it out loud. This way if the person says they handed you a twenty, show them the ten which is sitting right here on top of the tray. While pulling money out from your fingers under your tray, look at the bills and register in your mind what you are handing over to your customer.

Know exactly what change you are handing back to a customer.

- Don't let new coworkers use your server number for the till while training.

If there's a new person working, ask management to give her a distinct number or key right away. You don't want a new person using your number and getting used to it because if both girls end up working on the same shift, all drinks will be rung up under the same name and it could be quite the nightmare to try and figure out who owes what to the bar. Also, it keeps dishonest coworkers from ripping you off.

Keep your server number for ringing in drinks secret.

- If you start at a new bar or your bar has a price increase, print off a copy of the receipt with all the drinks and their prices you just punched in. Use this as your cheat sheet for a few weeks until you get accustomed to all the prices.

Not knowing prices of drinks by undercharging customers is another way of losing money.

• Pay close attention when handing the bartender money to buy small change or rolls of coin. A server is always thinking of numerous things at the same time and trying to stay a step ahead. Many times I have given the bartender forty dollars to buy a roll of loonies and three fives, only to grab my tray of drinks and run back onto the floor, forgetting about my money back at the bar.

When you give money to the bartender to buy small change, always double-check what you're handing over. Sometimes he's in a rush where he slips the money into the till only to say, "Did you give me $25 or $60?"

Pay attention to money you hand your bartender if you're buying rolls of coin or small bills.

• Forgetting to sign out on your shift is another way of losing money.

My shift is always the same, so I sign out part way through my shift or even at the beginning. If I know I might be leaving early or end up working overtime, I'll write myself a note and pop it into my box as a reminder to adjust the sign out sheet before I go home.

Remember to sign out before you go home or you worked that shift for free.

• Not knowing how to add up drinks properly in your head and shorting yourself frequently is another way of losing money. If you do this repeatedly, it will add up quickly.

Know how to count properly in your head.

- If you're going off shift, don't assume the customer wants to continue his tab with the other server. Many of my customers prefer to square up with me by making sure I am paid out on my tip and then they start a new tab with the new girl. I find some of my regulars leave me a bigger tip when I sign out with them than if I were to leave it to continue running with another server.

Give the customer a choice whether he wants to continue his tab with another server or to finish it up with you as you could end up with a bigger tip this way.

- Don't leave any loose paper money sitting on your tray as you run off to place an order in the kitchen, use the restroom, or deliver drinks to a table. If a scammer feels like they can get away with it without being noticed, they will make the move and take your money.

Don't trust anyone! Keep all paper money on you and your cash caddy full of coin clipped closed or a cloth sitting on your ashtray housing your coin to hide it.

The Fundamentals of Counting Money

The one thing that scared me the most when I looked into waitressing as a job many years ago was adding up prices of drinks in my head. I'm going to give you some useful tips to help you get over the same hurdle that has freaked out so many servers.

Practice Those Times Tables

Now is the time to learn your times tables if you didn't do it back in grade school. I'm not kidding! Practice counting while driving, watching TV, showering, etc. By learning to count quickly and accurately, you'll know how to calculate drinks efficiently in your head. Saving time means making more money! If you've never been good at math, now is the time to get better at it and it'll even keep you from losing money.

If you'll be working in a bar, it will be "cash and carry" most of the time and this is why you want to be good at adding up random prices of drinks in your head.

Add Your Drinks Up Properly

Over the years, I've been told by girls that when they add up drinks, they round up prices and tack on a couple of dollars just so they don't risk ripping themselves off. Don't get in the habit of this, as customers will eventually figure it out when another server charges them a lesser amount on the same round of drinks. You'll be looked at as the waitress who rips off customers and they'll never sit in your section or want to be served by you again. I assure you no waitress wants this kind of a reputation. Some customers will tell management and you can end up with a written warning or possibly even be fired because this is considered stealing.

It's Really Very Simple… Remember the Fundamentals

Here are some scenarios:

Two guys sit down and order two bottles of Kokanee at $5.90 each.
$5.90 + $5.90. Look at it as … Round up the price to $6.00.
$6.00 + $6.00 = $12.00. $12.00- $.10 from each beer.
$12-$.20=$11.80

A double Crown coke is $10.25 and a Kokanee is $5.95.
Look at it as $10.25 + $6.00 = $16.25–$.05 = $16.20

A round of 8 Kokanne beers at $5.90 each.
8 times $6.00 = $48.00
$48.00–$.80 ($.10 times 8 beer) = $47.20

Three beers at $5.75 each.
Look at it as $6.00 times 3 = $18.00
$18.00–$.75 ($.25 times 3 beer) = $17.25

Corona $6.50, coffee $4.00, pop $3.25, bottle water $4.00, Double Rum 10.25, Basket of Wings $10.00
Add up big numbers–$10.25 + $10.00 = $20.25
Then add up the same two numbers, then Corona and then the

water. $8.00 + $6.50 + $3.25 = $17.75
Then add up the two totals–$20.25 + $17.75 = $38.00

It's just an easier method of counting. It saves your time and brain power as well as makes sense in your head.

Adding Up Large Orders with Random Prices

If a large group comes in and orders several different drinks at different prices, write the full total on the back of your hand or a scrap sheet of paper. I could kick myself when I drop off twelve drinks and one person slaps down a hundred dollar bill and says, "I'll pay the first round." For large groups, you can even grab a small calculator and take it out onto the floor with you in case you need to quickly add up large amounts of random drinks.

I have dropped off large orders where a guy will say to me, "Ok, I'll pay for his drink, that guy's last three drinks, my food and the stag guy's food and the thirteen shots. Oh, and by the way, I need to do it immediately because my ride is here and I have to leave right away." I always have a pen or two clipped on the inside of my skirt so I can scribble down a few prices if I'm really stuck. Our bar has promo material lying around the bar on tables throughout the room and I'll grab a sheet and do my number scribbling on this if I'm stuck. If I'm desperately stuck for something to scribble on, I use a paper bill.

The most important advice I can give on this subject is that you should memorize those times tables and practice your counting. It does take time and the more you do it, the easier and faster it comes. Don't let this be your one hurdle keeping you from doing this job.

Romana's Story… Romana's First Day on the Job

My first serving job was selling shooters in a nightclub. I was terrified on my first day, thinking I'd look stupid by not knowing how to add up drinks or even end up losing money.

For the first two weeks, I carried a little security blanket on my tray; a tiny cheat sheet that gave me some confidence. As I think back, *it's a little funny because it was only adding up multiples of $3.75! My tiny cheat sheet read:*

1 shooter — $3.75
2" — $7.50
3" — $11.25
4" — $15.00
5" — $18.75
6" — $22.50
7" — $26.25
8" — $30.00

Twenty years later, I'm pretty quick at counting odd prices in my head, thanks to my husband Rod! He taught me the art of fundamentals and how easy counting in your head can actually be.

The Memorizing Secret

I'm always being asked by customers how I manage to remember so many drinks at one time in my head. There really isn't any magic to it as I just do it and I'm good at it because I've been doing it for over twenty years. That's my secret: just lots of practice.

I was trained over fifteen years ago to memorize all of my food and drink orders and I'm glad I was forced to learn this way because it has made me more efficient over the years. For example, when a customer is talking to me, instead of stopping to write an order down, I'm grabbing for empties at the same time or wiping their table while listening to them. I'm able to point at drinks and do the "thumbs up" signal if I am being waved at for another round and if my free hand is full, I'm still able to nod or mouth "Okay" when needing to communicate with someone while I'm passing by. I'm doing all this at the same time while registering all these drinks in my head. A good server definitely has to be good at multi-tasking.

The Advantages of Memorization

My tray is *stuck* to my left arm. What I mean by stuck is that my tray does not leave my arm. It does not get set down on a table until I loop around the room and end up back at the bar/waitress station.

I don't like to set my tray down on a table because people can accidentally kick into the table resulting in drinks sloshing and spilling on or off my tray. I can accidentally tip my tray over by setting it down and the bottom side can get sticky and wet. The drinks are exposed to customers who can slip something in there (drugs) while my head is turned and I'm not paying attention. My change is visible for anyone to help themselves to if I remove my rag to turn around and give a table a wipe. By hoisting my tray up and then setting it down constantly, I'm wasting valuable time and wearing out my shoulder. . With that tray stuck on my arm, my right hand is free to grab empties and garbage, wipe tables, push in chairs, deal with money or touch people on their back if I'm passing by so they know I'm there (this way they won't get up or move back, knocking into my tray). I can fly around the room pointing at drinks, using hand signals or even waving at customers as they enter or leave the room. I'm extremely talented at giving one-arm hugs with a full tray of drinks without spilling a drop!

When I loop around the room and end up back at the till, the first thing I do is start punching my drinks into the till. Then, I spin around and take a look at my room to see if there's anyone I've forgotten. I like to backtrack and think about all the drink orders I've taken. If I'm really busy, I'll add four to six extra drinks that are on special to my order. This way, if there's anyone I forgot or some new bodies who entered the room, I have extra beer to sell.

I have coworkers who would rather jot down drinks as they move through the room. If you're new or haven't used the memorizing system before and you'd prefer to write down your orders, then write them down. You want to use whatever is easier and less stressful for you, especially during the busy times. I suggest during the slower times, you get into the habit of stretching your mind and work on your memorization. Make it a mission to work a full shift while memorizing everything. It will make you a stronger server.

Write Down the Random Information

Many times I'll drop off drinks and a customer tells me he has no money on him because he needs to grab some out of the debit machine. I'll point to where the ATM machine is located and mention I'll collect money next time I walk by. This way it puts the pressure on him to have my money ready for me the next time I'm by. I make sure to jot down a quick note to myself on a scrap piece of paper. JUG, TBL 32 seems to do the trick for me. Many times I would try and rely on my memory to collect, but I get busy and side tracked with other things. When I drive home at night or lay in bed, IT pops into my head … the guy who owed me for the Stoli coke at table nine or the guys who owe me money for the two cheeseburgers at table thirty-two. Of course, some people don't stop and remind you, "I owe you money." The honest people do, but there are those who won't or they may have forgotten as well. It's my responsibility to collect my money so I can only blame myself if I forget.

Try to stay organized so you don't have to concentrate on remembering every random thing. Anything you should know for a later time, such as staff meeting dates, schedule changes and supplies you've run out of, write it down on a piece of paper and pop it into your waitress box so you don't have to memorize it.

For coworkers and dancers who owe you money for food or drinks during your shift, put their name on one small sheet of paper as a reminder and keep it in a glass near the till. I put it in list form with the name and amount due and I cross off the people as they pay me. This way, I can put away any unnecessary paperwork, such as food bills and get them out of my way and it keeps the till area rather clutter-free. By writing down random information, it saves your brain power to remember drink and food orders and even to learn customer's names!

At the beginning of the week, get in the habit of rechecking the schedule. Even if you've worked the same shift for years, people go on holidays, quit, or get fired unexpectedly or there's some other last-minute emergency change. If you were scheduled and didn't show up for your scheduled shift, you will be to blame. You know what they say … *never assume—It makes an ass out of u and me.* By writing stuff down, you don't have to rely on your memory all the time.

If you don't carry a day timer, you can get a small one at the dollar store or use your cell phone. It's extremely handy to keep track of your personal life as well as anything to do with work (staff meetings, promoting trips, special functions, change of shifts, etc).

Over twenty years ago, I had four jobs going at one time. My day timer was my best friend at that time and it kept my life organized so I didn't have to think too much about where I was supposed to be and when. I just had to remember to check my day-timer the night before.

Master the Till and Store the Popular PLUs in Your Mind

When you're new to a job and familiarizing yourself with a new till, you'll struggle with it in the beginning. By using it regularly, you gain speed in finding your items in the till quickly. During slow times, play with it to become knowledgeable about it. The faster you ring in your drink orders, the quicker you get them from the bartender and deliver them to your customers. By learning to punch in your orders quickly and in proper sequence, you make your bartender's job easier and you don't hold up the other servers who are in line behind you.

In order to save time, memorize as many PLUs as you can. A PLU is a code number for an item in some tills. If I want to ring in a Crown Royal, I would look for it under the rye button. All the rye we sell would be listed there with their own code numbers under alphabetical order. I have many PLUs memorized for the most popular premium drinks we sell as well as local bottles of beer.

It's a great idea to memorize food prices as well. This way it saves you time when you add up bills or you can help out a customer when they ask you how much an item costs. It comes in extremely handy when you want to get a customer to prepay for a food item when you work the nightshift.

Some Memorization Tips

If you've never memorized drink or food orders, all it really takes is practice. The more you do it, the easier it gets. To this day, customers are absolutely amazed I can remember an entire tray of drinks and know one cocktail from another.

- If you want to try memorizing food, start easy on yourself. Try with one customer first. Move onto two, three, and then a whole table of people. It really is not that hard when you practice and do it a lot. Take your orders and file them in your mind. In the beginning, have a pen and scrap paper as a security blanket just in case you start to lose control and start to forget.

- If you work on the art of memorizing drink orders, you'll be more successful at this job and make more money. There's nothing wrong with writing down orders, but when a server does, she spends much of her time writing when she could be doing other tasks at the same time.

- As I head towards the bar, I'm thinking about the loop around the room I just did. I'm starting to rearrange all the drinks I have stored in my head. I'm doing a calculation of how many bottles of Miller or how many Coronas I need. If I have an estimate of needing seven pints of beer, I take out a couple extra in case I forgot anyone. I will pack out nine as I can always sell a couple extra pints to new people if they happen to enter the bar.

- You want to figure out an easy system for yourself. Remember when you were in school and you had to memorize stuff for an exam? I thought of the craziest things to get something to stick in my mind. I still use this system to this day. Here are a few examples of memorizing I use:

1. *A customer orders a clubhouse on brown with a salad and ranch dressing. I don't repeat to myself in my head, clubhouse on brown with a salad and ranch dressing. I shorten it and*

say to myself… club, brown, ranch. I know it's a clubhouse on brown with salad.

2. *A customer orders a steak sandwich, medium rare with Caesar salad. I just think to myself, MY steak. This is exactly the way I would order a steak for myself. If a steak is ordered well done, I picture the guy's face almost blackened. I use visualization when I can.*

3. *When someone orders a bacon cheeseburger with fries, I just think burger. This is the most common way customers order their burgers. If he were to order, no tomato, just think burger, no tomato. If a plain burger is ordered, I think naked burger.*

4. *A customer orders a pulled pork sandwich. I visualize him pulling my hair!*

5. *An order of hot wings, I imagine his head blowing up from the hot sauce.*

- It can get a little hairy when a table of customers ask for specifics such as a side of mayo, extra guacamole, no onions, and so forth.

- If you forget a customer's food order by the time you get to your till, just run back and ask him again. People understand when you are busy, so don't sweat it and move on. If you dwell on it, you'll end up getting yourself flustered and go into a pattern of forgetting more orders.

- For a large party of customers, I will pull out a pen and scrap paper to write down the order just so I keep it all straight. I know I won't be able to remember twelve different meals on top of a head full of drinks. I'm good at my job, but I'm also not Superwoman!

Chapter 4
Different Strategies of Speed

A Typical Slammed Night For a Cocktail Waitress

Picture this … It's a pretty mellow night as you're cruising along serving your customers. You've got a moment or two to chat with regulars, gossip a bit with your bartender and even cruise into the kitchen to help out by scraping old food off the dirty dishes and running them through the dishwasher.

Six new customers walk in, they ask for menus and a round of drinks. You saunter to the bar and grab their order. After dropping it off, you pass by a small group of young men who just sat down at the next table over. After asking them for their identification and waiting patiently while they pull out their wallets, you take their order. Continuing around the room, a few more tables want rounds, Andy asks you for more ketchup and napkins, Jim would like a glass of ice water and all the while you're grabbing empties, pushing in chairs and wiping tables. Stopping at table thirty three, you scoop the large amount of change onto your tray that was left for you as a tip and pick up the last empties. While wiping the table, you notice the amount of bodies entering the bar is starting to increase rather quickly and you feel the energy level in the room start to rise.

Back at the bar you ring up your order and then unload the empties and garbage off your tray. You decide to add six extra beers that are on sale to your tray because the number of people entering the bar is steadily increasing and you know you'll easily sell them. Quickly, you load your tray and then heave your full tray onto your arm and off you go. Oops! You forgot a mug of water and menus so you backtrack towards the bar.

Heading back out onto the floor with your full tray, water, and menus, you notice a new group hooting and hollering while strolling into the room. The guy dressed in a tacky dirty wedding dress is looking rather sheepish—a stag. You glance at the large party heading to the stage. You pick up your speed, dropping off drinks, grabbing empties and pushing in chairs which are scattered in your way, while staying on the map of the room so you don't miss anyone.

Table five now wants their bill and is asking if you could please call them a taxi. A punk at table seven has his feet propped up on his table while busy texting on his cell phone as you abruptly push his feet off while walking by. He yells, "What the hell?!" before you ask him if he'd mind you coming to his house and sticking your feet up on his kitchen table. He gives you a dumb vacant look as you shake your head and continue towards gyno, noticing the neighbourhood drunk falling asleep. Shaking him awake, you warn him that you'll be asking him to leave if you have to wake him a second time.

As you walk around gyno, Mike hands you thirty dollars and says, "Here Ro. I owe you for three beers. Keep the change!" You smile and wave at him as he runs out the door.

A new group of young people now sit at table twelve and bicker with you as to why you're asking them for ID. You tell them you don't have time to argue and demand they either pull out two pieces of identification or leave. As your tray arm starts to shake from the weight, they further waste your time by asking what the cheapest alcoholic drink being sold is and then ask you to name all the specials. Two kids tell you they have no money and you let them know they all have to order a drink or they have to leave. They decide to get up and exit, leaving all their chairs strewn about. While pushing in the chairs that are in your way, you feel your blood start to boil while thinking of the valuable time they just wasted. Your arm feels like it's going to fall off now.

Glancing at the bar, you notice the party from table five is standing at the bar, patiently waiting for you so they can square up and pay their bill. You haven't made it to the stag party yet sitting at gyno who seem to be getting rowdier by the minute. You scream,

"Stop!" as you suddenly freeze and hold your foot out to stop a drunken girl from backing into your tray because both hands are unavailable to block her.

Wayne waves you over and tells you he has just got to tell you this great joke he heard yesterday. You try to keep calm as you politely tell him you're really busy right now and you'd love to hear it when you've got a spare moment.

You make it to the stag guys and they order every different drink under the sun that seems to range from a Miller, Stella, Rum coke with three cubes of ice and two lime twists, a Bombay tonic, coke neat, coffee with three sacks of sugar, a double Crown ginger short, Smirnoff Ice with a set up, Grey Goose water with a shot of cranberry juice, and what was that last drink ordered? You've got a guy in the group asking you how much a private dance costs and another guy informs you the group is starving and wants to order food right away. The big shot in the group wearing the sunglasses mentions, "Could you bring out a dozen shots of Cuervo right away?" As you listen to him order, you wonder if he's stoned, in hiding, trying to look cool or is just stupid. You decide on all of the above.

As you head to the bar, your arm is singing with the pain of dragging your tray of empties around the room. You wonder where the party at table five went to. Hopefully, just to the restroom or out for a smoke. You don't panic because you remind yourself you've served this group many times in the past and they always leave a handsome tip.

You notice a twenty dollar bill lying on the floor. With a shaky arm, you set your full tray down on the empty table beside it and retrieve it off the floor. You stretch the sore muscles in your arm before picking up your heavy tray of empties again and balancing it on your arm. You finally make it back to the till.

Glancing at your bartender, you notice he's pouring and serving his line as quickly as possible and you hate to tell him the glass washer is full and you have no room to add any more dirty glasses to it unless he starts to unload it.

Punching in your next orders, you realize you won't be able to carry it all out. You run out the three jugs and glassware and quickly mumble to the group you'll be right back for money. As you stand there punching in your order, a few regulars are leaving for the night and have brought their empty bottles up to the bar for you. You thank them as they put the empty bottles in the proper beer case.

You try to keep your cool as you feel the panic rise. More people are walking in the room; a group of regulars are asking which section of the room you're working and if you could please bring out their usual drinks right away. A group of your regular bad boys come in right after, hug you, and ask if there's an available table for them. You tell them they can sit at the staff table with the staff reserved sign on it and you'll be out with their usual drinks right away. You know it's turning into a great night for making tips, even though you'll be dealing with a sore back, aching shoulder and swollen feet later.

Glancing at the time, you realize another server won't be on for another hour and the doorman who checks identification at the door won't start for another hour as well.

You feel like you're losing control. You start to sweat and shake and … STOP!! You've been slammed! You're only human and there's only so much you can do.

First, punch in all the drinks you remember. Look back at the room, retrace your steps, and punch in any drinks that were not thought of. As the bartender starts loading the counter with all drinks, grab another tray and run out drinks to regulars on tabs and close by (this saves room on your tray). While running back to the bar, only gather empties from deserted tables because people will continue to order from you and you definitely won't have any room on your tray to add more drinks. If customers try stopping you, respond with "I'll be with you in a moment!"

When taking out your full tray, while waiting for customers to pull out money, ask people at the next table if they need another round and grab their empties—use those precious moments.

When you get slammed, carry as many extra drinks as you can since you'll always get rid of them and the bottles don't take up too much room on your tray. Depending on the crowd, I carry extra pints and bottles on special since they're a hot seller and are a cheap price. This way, if someone who just came into the bar asks you for a Canadian, you can say, "I have an extra Budweiser on my tray you can have right now if you don't want to wait for me to run to the bar and it's on sale." Nine times out of ten, he'll buy it just so he doesn't have to wait for you to come back or he has to go to the bar and stand in the line up. Believe me, you'll have a table buy all the extra beer you have on your tray because some people are power drinking and they get caught up in the moment and love to show off.

Full Tray OUT / Full Tray IN

When you're busy, the rule is FULL TRAY OUT/ FULL TRAY IN. When you take a bottle of beer off your tray, replace the spot with an empty. Turn the bottle around so you can't see the label and this symbolizes an empty. By stacking empty glasses into one another or empty bottles into pint mugs or jugs, this saves room on your tray for more empties.

If you really feel out of control, your room is beginning to look like a mess and you're starting to run out of clean glassware, ask for help. Ask someone like the shooter girl or DJ if they have a spare moment to grab a bus pan and fly through the room to grab empties. Make sure you remember to slip them some money, since no one likes to work for free. They'll be more than happy to help you out the next time you need it.

I could bang my head against the wall when I see servers walk past a table littered with empties and run to the till to ring in orders with an empty tray. This is where I take a look at her section and see how many empties are laying around on tables and around the stage area. Servers need to stay on top of cleanliness because when there are numerous amounts of empties down at the stage, there's more of a chance a dancer can kick into them. They'll break and shoot out into the audience when she swings around the pole while doing her pole tricks. Keep empties from accumulating on tables because it looks messy and they get in a customer's way. Eventually, the bartender will run out of clean glassware too. There won't be room on a table if the guys ordered meals since tables in bars are not big to begin with.

If you stay focused and move quickly, you'll do just fine. When you panic, you feel like throwing down your tray and running from the room. Before you know it, help arrives, your room gets back to being orderly and your heart rate comes back down to normal from panic mode.

Customers are usually pretty understanding, so if someone asks you why it's taking so long for drinks or looks like they're getting annoyed with the amount of time it's taking for you to deliver their order, open your mouth and tell them you're the only waitress on the floor right now. Usually they'll understand and feel empathy for you. On the other hand, if someone is rude, tell them you're doing the best you can and maybe they should go to the bar for their drinks. Remember, you can't please everyone.

If you're working with another server and the bar gets overly busy where you can't keep up, you can always ask her to take over some of your tables. I'm usually pretty happy to help out a fellow server when asked because its extra money I can make and I love being busy to the point of where my shift feels like it's flying by.

People will get up and go to the bar to buy a drink if they see you're too busy and not coming around fast enough. If you can't keep up any longer to drink orders, tell customers nearest the bar you're extremely busy right now and it would be a lot quicker for them to get their first round of drinks at the bar and apologize for this. They'll appreciate your honesty and it will relieve some of the pressure off you.

"Selling booze pays the bills" is what I always hear in my head from my first manager, Mary, who hired and trained me. If you get slammed, leave the wiping and move the chairs in your way. Grab empties as you run along, cramming garbage into empty jugs or pint mugs. Hang a couple of empty jugs from the fingers under your tray if you run out of room on your tray or in your free hand. Leave dishes; you can always run out next time around and stack a pile on top of each other and take them away in one swoop or you can even ask the DJ or shooter girl to do you a favour and clear them away. Pick up your speed, stay focused, keep organized and you'll manage just fine.

When you're remembering all drinks, flying through the room dropping off cocktails and beer, collecting money, staying on top of your empties, wiping tables, and pushing in chairs, it's an exhilarating feeling! You know you're doing a great job when customers are tipping you like crazy (you can't wait to count your tips at the end of the shift) and patrons are commenting on what a great job you're doing.

Manage Your Time Efficiently

Every server will encounter times when she gets slammed and she feels the panic starting to rise. You get so bombarded with drink orders you wonder if you'll be able to fit them all on your tray and carry them all out. Will the customers still be there by the time you come back around? You feel like you need to almost break into a run but you need to keep your cool and stay focused. You'll get there when you get there. If the customers disappear, you'll resell the drinks to someone else; "no big deal," you tell yourself.

When the bartender starts making your drinks, help him out by putting straws and lime twists into them, then arrange the drinks on your tray very tight together. If there are tables nearby who just ordered (and these customers have open tabs), grab those drinks and run them over to the table in your hands or a separate tray (leave your original tray at the bar). I'll interrupt with a "Sorry to interrupt guys!" as I drop off the drinks and leave again quickly. By the time you return to the bar, place more drinks on your tray. Running out drinks to nearby tables saves room on your tray, it's less weight to carry and the drinks are delivered quicker, which equals more tips.

If you have a jug or two for a table, run out the jugs and empty glasses. I will stack glasses into one another and carry them all in one hand. Tell the group, "Guys, I'll be back in a couple of minutes for money." If you think you'll forget to collect money as you pass by their table, jot down a quick note for yourself. I'll write JUG,

TBL 39. This reminds me to collect money for a jug at table 39. If a patron has left the table to go smoke, use the restroom, answer his phone or use the ATM machine and you dropped off a drink without payment, make a quick note to collect money the next time you pass by. Don't always rely on your memory for random things when you're busy. On my drive home after work on a Friday night, I remembered the girl at table twenty-three who owed me for a Caesar, but I forgot to collect from her because she went to use the ATM. I don't know about you but if I'm going to pay for anyone's drink, I'd prefer to pay for a friend's and not a stranger's.

As I've said before, if you notice new people coming into the bar, carry extra drinks. If bottles of Canadian are on sale, carry an extra four to six extras on your tray. If you don't sell them during this trip around the bar, then maybe you'll get rid of them on the next. If they still haven't sold, give them to the bartender to put on ice. Make sure you write yourself a note you are up those beers.

Customers love it when they sit down and you tell them you have extra bottles on your tray they can purchase now, instead of waiting for you to go all the way to the bar. They'll usually buy the beer on your tray, instead of waiting for their beer of choice. I like to joke around and say I knew they were coming in the door, and I purposely planned for them to get the beer right away. If you joke around and make it fun, you'll put them in an even better mood than what they were in and usually receive a very nice tip!

Friday afternoons are really busy. Not just for my bar, but for most pubs. The blue collar workers get off of work for the week and enjoy a couple beers with their buddies, and some will only have a certain amount of time to kill before they have to go home to their families. Some of these guys are on a drinking frenzy, so the quicker you serve them, the more drinks are bought. Higher sales mean you look good to the boss and you make more tips!

Speed is important in this industry. Customers don't want to see you sauntering around the room at a slow pace when the room is buzzing. When the lunch or dinner rush starts to pick up, I increase the pace of my walk and everything I do is with speed and consistency. My walk has a purpose and I don't mosey around or wander aimlessly as I want to get around the room or my section quickly. This way, customers see my face more often and know the drink they ordered will arrive quickly, so they won't be as inclined to get up and go to the bartender or move to another server's section for better service. If they go to the bar for the rest of the night, it's bad for you because it's a table you aren't making any money off of and you're stuck picking up all the empties and cleaning up after them. After all, I'm there to make money, so I want people to keep me busy and order their drinks only from me. The quicker you serve your customers, the quicker they drink and the quicker they'll leave. This quick turnover of customers means new ones will replace the previous and you continue making more money in tips.

Stay on top of your efficiency because this is the time to make some money. Before you know it, the room empties and you can go back to slowing down your pace. Keep this in mind for any rush that occurs during your shift at any time of day or night. It may happen that a party will sit at one of your tables for a longer time than usual and sip on their one drink. This is a waiting game with this type of customer and you have to wait for them to leave. Before you know it, they'll be gone and a new group will be there keeping you busy and making you money.

Saving Time

I always keep my mind open to new ways on saving time. Any time saved is used to sell drinks, which means more money for the bar (higher sales—you look good in the boss's eyes) and tips for yourself (the main reason why you're there in the first place).

Know About All the Daily Specials

Before starting your shift, check on all the drink and food specials. Take a walk into the kitchen and find out the special of the day or daily soup is. During this time, the cook will let you know if the kitchen is out of wings or there are only ten steaks left until the afternoon delivery order comes in.

It looks unprofessional when a customer asks what the soup of the day is and the server has no idea. Then she has to walk into the kitchen and make an unnecessary trip to find out and dash back out to the customer.

Take Initiative and Make Use of Every Second

When the room is humming, all staff is busy doing something. As your bartender puts all the bottles on the counter, start popping the caps open yourself and place them on your tray. Try to stay one step ahead of him to help him out. Put limes in your Corona bottles and drinks, and place your straws in as well. Not only are you helping him out, you're helping yourself out by getting drinks ready to go on your tray quicker. This gets you in and out of the bar immediately.

The rule is when you fill a beer case up, don't leave it there for someone else to get rid of; move it! It's annoying when you come up to the bar with a full tray of empties and you've got to start moving full cases of empties out of the way. When unloading any empty bottles from your tray, tip each one upside down over the sink to get any leftover liquid out. Then place it into the case. If you put bottles into the case with liquid inside, when someone goes to move the case and it drops slightly, they get splashed in the face or their shirt with stale beer.

Don't slam empty bottles in the case. It's easy to start hurrying when you get busy and rush by slamming bottles. In turn, they chip at the mouth area and glass can fly. I've almost been shot in the eye this way a couple times. When you put the bottles into the case, stack them neatly from the beginning because when it gets busy, you don't want to waste time re-stacking and organizing them.

If the glass washer is full, turn it on and run the dirty glassware through. On busy nights, the glass washer will be kept turned on most of the time anyways.

As you walk the floor, get in the habit of organizing your coin, folding loose bills into your fingers and reorganizing the bottles or glasses on your tray to make room for more empties.

I work with some great girls. When I arrive at the till and one of my girls isn't that busy, she'll start unloading my tray for me while I ring up my orders. When I have a packed tray, girls will offer to run out drinks for me if I need to. It's great working with such an awesome team of people. We love to help each other out when we can.

What to Do if You Forget a Drink

"Sorry, I AM human, and I WILL forget a drink or two!" I catch myself reminding an upset customer about this once in a while.

If you find you are having a hard time memorizing drink orders, do yourself a favour and get yourself a cash caddy and notepad so you can write down your orders. It'll prevent you from becoming more stressed out when you get busy and you can stay focused and concentrate on getting your job done without any customer complaints.

I use an ashtray as my coin holder, so I don't have a place to set a notepad. No matter how busy I get, I will memorize until my brain is at the point of almost exploding. Since day one, I was trained to memorize all drinks because all servers weren't allowed to write anything down so this is what I'm used to. I like this method because it's challenging and my hands are free to wipe tables, push in chairs, and move drinks and empties on and off my tray as I cruise around the room.

I don't forget too many drinks, but when I get slammed, it has happened. I have a few remarks I use on guys if I happen to forget their drinks. It keeps them from getting too upset with me and it keeps the mood light and fun.

First off, I apologize profusely and then I throw in, "I always seem to forget all the good looking guys!" This makes them smile and if I'm busy, usually the returned comment is, "That's ok. We can see you're really busy."

I respond with "Oh good! Then I can forget you guys again?" as I wink at them. At this point, I'll have all the empties on my tray so I quickly return to the bar to grab their drinks and deliver them right away. If my tray still has drinks to deliver to others, I keep on my map of the room and drop them off. As soon as I return to the bar, I grab the drinks that slipped my mind and run them out to the forgotten ones. Then I zip back to the bar for the rest of my order and get back on track.

A word of advice… when I forget someone's drink, I try not to panic and dwell on it because, if I do, I'll end up forgetting other people and it turns into this vicious cycle of forgetting more and more drinks. I'll get myself so stressed out and start to feel like I'm out of control and falling apart.

If I forget a customer's drink and they're extremely rude about it and I can tell by their attitude that they just won't let it go, I say to them, "Sorry, but I'm only human and I do forget a drink now and then. I suggest that next time you go get your drink at the bar." I'm not mean about it and I don't wait for a response. I walk away and continue doing my job. He'll be able to tell by my reaction that I'm busy and have plenty of other people to serve.

Sometimes customers joke back at me when I ask if they want another drink. They'll usually tease me and say, "Should I order now in case you forget my drink again?" or, "Are you going to forget me again?"

I usually just smile and respond with, "Guess we'll have to wait and see!"

Another comment the guys make is, "Ok, if you forget me again, you're paying for my next beer, right?"

I respond with, "Ok, It's a deal!"

Another way to save the moment with a customer if you keep forgetting their drink is to buy them one. I've gotten so busy while my poor regular sits there patiently as I run by him two times, only to forget him yet again. At this point, I'll leave my tray at the bar, run the beer out and drop it off saying, "Jim, I'm so sorry! Your first one is on me!" It doesn't happen very often but this has happened a couple times.

Sometimes, the patron will stop me as I run by and he'll try to pay for the drink. I refuse and the bill is usually thrown onto my tray as he says, "Ro, then please keep it as a tip!" Other times, the money is left under their empty glass when they leave.

We used to do a lunch draw during our lunch rush on the dayshift. If I would forget a drink or if it was someone's birthday, I would give them an extra lunch draw ticket or two, to up their chance of winning the draw.

Many years ago, I was at a nightclub and I ordered a sambucca paralyser. I waited almost twenty minutes until the server finally returned. She was extremely busy and said, "I'm sorry. I'll have to go get you another drink. Yours tipped off my tray and fell onto the floor." I will never know if the drink was spilled or was forgotten. I know I would have been more upset if she said she had forgotten it. I'll have to remember to try this excuse when I get slammed and forget a drink for someone.

If you forget a pint or jug of beer, you can say the bartender is tapping the keg. If a coffee drink is forgotten, tell the customer the bartender is making a fresh pot. If you forget a cocktail, you can say the pop is out on the gun and the bartender is changing it. If you forget a bottle of beer, you can mention the bar ran out and it'll be a moment until the bartender goes to the cooler to retrieve another case. You don't want to get in the habit of telling customers little white lies, but in a pinch use these to keep a customer from getting too upset and to keep yourself sane.

If you forget a drink or forget to put a food order into the kitchen, spill a drink on someone, or any other mistake, always over- apologize. If you try your best to save the moment and the customer is just being plain rude, remember you can't please everyone and personalities do clash. If you just can't save the situation, this is a time where you can ask another server to switch tables with you as a last resort.

If you find you're having a hard time keeping up to your section, ask another server if she would like to take over some of your tables. Many times the new girls ask me to do this and I'm glad to make the extra, unexpected money. It keeps the other server from getting too frazzled and the customers are happy, especially if they're on a drinking binge.

Chapter 5
Downtime

Helping Coworkers

When Your Section is Dead

Any server can get antsy and frustrated during the periods when she sees her coworkers loading their trays and running back out to their sections, while she strolls through hers barely making a sale. Your sleepy section seems to contain customers who want to take it easy and nurse their drink and others are just killing time with one beer before the nightclub opens next door. Any customers who you talk to seem to wave you away and say, "We're leaving after this drink, thanks." As you scan and look over at the other server's section, it looks like it's busy and humming along.

This is discouraging for any server who ends up with mellow non-drinkers in her section, especially when the rest of the room is so alive and busy. The only thing I can suggest is to keep any unoccupied tables clean and inviting to newcomers who enter.

Think positive and hopefully the non-drinkers will get tired of hanging around and leave. A turnover in new people will transpire and you'll start humming along again too.

Keep Yourself Busy During the Slow Times

During any slow periods, I like to keep busy because it makes the time go by quicker. I like to take a walk into the kitchen and see if dirty plates need food scraped off of them and then put onto the dish rack. Then I rinse them off and run them through the dishwasher. On a busy night, I will take a walk into the restroom to pick up any dirty glasses which happen to make their way in there.

Never neglect your section for more than three minutes at a time. As you walk through your section, keep an eye out for new customers, customers wanting another drink and others wanting their tabs.

Don't walk into another server's section and stand there gabbing with customers. It doesn't look very professional and you just end up getting in her way.

Help Out Your Fellow Server

I'll ask the other servers if they want me to walk through their section and pick up any empties starting to accumulate. I'll pick up any dirty dishes, condiments, used napkins and cutlery. I grab my wet rag and give the table a quick wipe, especially if there is spilled food or drink. The customer will appreciate it and so will the server. If customers want to order from me, I let them know their server will be with them momentarily as I'm only there helping out by picking up empties. Push in all chairs and straighten tables if they're out of position.

Many years ago, I used to work with a server who, when she came onto the floor to start her shift, always started by walking through my section first by collecting all my empties and then continuing over to her side taking her customers' orders. In the history of my serving career, she was the only server who ever did this and I can't express how thoughtful and helpful this was! She was one hell of an awesome server with an infectious laugh and so fun to work with. Thank you May!

If you're standing around at the bar while waiting for drinks and a server comes up with a full tray of empties, unload it for her so she can punch in her next order into the till.

If a fellow server has an extremely large order, offer to carry any drinks out for her and drop them off. Mention to the customer their server will be around in a moment to collect money from them.

Help Out the Bartender

I'll jump behind the bar and help out my bartender if he's getting behind. Some bars don't allow other staff behind the bar, so find out your bar rules about this.

The glass washer always needs unloading. Check if the ice well needs refilling and if any beer or coolers need restocking. Look at the sugar and coffee supplies if they need refilling as well. Check to see if the straws need topping up or if he's low on lime wedges or other garnishes. There is *always* something that can be done.

Helping out all coworkers is important as you may need the favour returned one day.

Preparation for the Busy Shifts

For many of us, the slow periods during some of our shifts may get to the point of being so inactive and mundane they become the boredom blues.

During my daily lunch rushes, I enjoy having a purpose and being busy while running out drinks and serving food. Before long, it slows down to the point of where the room empties out; the blue collar workers take off back to work, the students taking the first aid course who were on a lunch break return to school across the street and the random single guys have disappeared to get on with their day.

It's these slow, inactive periods when I like to make good use of time and get random tasks done around the room so I don't end up dealing with the annoying boredom blues.

Clean Up the Room

When the rush ends, the first thing on the agenda is to clean my room and put things back to normal. Empties are picked up and put away while dirty glasses are run through the glass washer. All condiments are put away, dirty dishes are taken to the kitchen where all leftover food is scraped into the trash can and the plates are stacked onto the wash rack and rinsed off. The tables are straightened if moved out of position and then given a thorough wipe while all chairs are pushed in and any promotional material is reset on top.

As new customers enter the room and sit down, I stop what I'm doing and walk over to serve them immediately. After they have a drink on the table and maybe a menu in hand, I return to where I left off. If they're looking at a menu, I don't forget to check on them in a couple of minutes to take their food order.

There is never a time when a server should be standing around yawning and complaining, "I'm bored." If you're all caught up with tidying the room, look around and you'll always find chores to keep you busy.

Speed Up Your Cash-out

As long as I'm by myself at the till and there are no customers milling around me, I like to unlock my waitress box and organize all my paper bills. I stack all the bills in the same direction with the same side up, separating all denominations. If I have a large stack, I'll count up my twenties and slip a rubber band around every five hundred or thousand dollars. I stack together all my visa and interact slips as well as any promo tabs or pull tabs. Since I've saved some time by doing most of the grunt work of organizing my money and slips earlier on in my shift, I can leave earlier.

Sometimes customers move to the other side of the room to see a friend or move to another chair which is more comfortable. Because of this, they may order shooters from the shooter girl or the rest of their drinks from another server. This means other servers are putting drinks or food on his bill and when he pays his tab and leaves a tip, it's only fair to split the tip amongst the servers who served him. The slow period is the time where I like to work out any tips owed to other servers on all of my closed tabs. It's really quite easy and not hard at all to figure out. By working out tips on tabs during the slow parts of your shift, you don't have to do it at the end of your shift when you're itching to get your cash done and go home.

Other Jobs

- Periodically, I like to help out the bartender and we go through all glassware. Taking a clean, wet rag, I re-wipe all glass wear, beer glasses, beer mugs, shooter glasses, martini glasses and wine glasses. I'll hold them up to the light and inspect them for greasy finger prints, lipstick on rims, coffee rings, dark foggy type of discoloration from cola and reddish tinge from clamato or tomato juice that's added to beer or Caesars.

It's not unusual to find a coating of cinnamon inside some of the shooter glasses from the China White shooters. About once a month I take all our plastic beer jugs into the kitchen, pour some bleach and hot water into them, let them sit for 20 minutes and then run them through the dishwasher in the kitchen. This gets rid of any discoloration scrubbing by hand doesn't help. The glass washer does a pretty good job cleaning and disinfecting, but it takes some elbow grease to get rid of the hard stuff.

- As most servers are in a rush to leave at the end of their shift, the only attention trays are usually given is a quick wipe with a dirty cloth so it's a good idea to give them a thorough clean every day. Sprinkling baking soda and pouring hot water on trays with a cork liner helps to neutralize the foul odour that accumulates from alcohol spilling on them during a shift. Grab a glass, flip it upside down and scrub the soda into the cork. Finish up by rinsing it away with warm water and dry with a clean cloth. The baking soda is great to use on any tray.

- Our shooter girls have plastic, glow-in-the-dark trays with a removable rubber tray liner. They take it apart and run both pieces through the glass washer. Over time the rubber liner starts to crinkle up and harden and doesn't sit flat against the tray any longer. When this occurs, the shooter glass won't sit flat and it can tip and spill when the girl walks with it. Not too long ago, my bartender decided to take the tray and its rubber liner into the kitchen. He held it under the salamander (this is the heating element that melts cheese quickly on nachos) to heat up the liner for a minute and this is what flattened it to the point of functioning like new again … ingenious!

- Trays holding random glassware are sprayed and wiped with a cleaner, while the rubber mats are run through the glass washer.

- We have spray bottles containing glass cleaner, deodorizer and sanitizer. It is used at the end of the night to spray down all tables. I like to fill up all bottles when I have some time to kill.

- Mirrors or glass in the room that looks foggy, dirty, or contains fingerprints are cleaned during slow periods as well.

- Cleaning and de-cluttering once a week around the till is a good idea because by Saturday night there are too many lipsticks, perfume bottles and odds and ends collected in a glass.

Every Tuesday I collect it all up and put it into the staff room. Then I wipe down the till, the phone, visa machine and any other machinery that may have dust, dirt, or spills on it. The sink is given a good scrub every couple of days with a handy little brush I picked up at the dollar store and sanitizer. The soap dispenser is filled when low.

- I refill the stapler if needed and check stock on any guest cheques, till tape and coasters that may be running low.

- Going through the laminated kitchen menus, I check if they're sticky or covered in ketchup or other food. They're given a good wipe with a clean wet cloth and then dried with a dry one. Do not use a spray cleaner since it makes the menus stick together and they feel tacky to the touch.

- Take a look at the chairs in your bar and see if they need a wash down or the crumbs and dirt wiped out from the grooves. Look at the foot rests on the bar stools as many get caked with mud and grime from dirty work boots. Cleaning with a bucket filled with warm water and soap and a clean cloth works wonders.

Don't forget to dry with a clean cloth as you don't want new customers sitting in wet chairs.

• I like everyday chores to be effortless and tools to be easily accessible around the bar. So to accomplish this, many times I take initiative myself to organize items and get things done. Many years ago when our bar did renovating, they put in new lights with a nice big section of twenty-five light switches. When lights around the room needed to be dimmed or brightened quickly, you didn't know which switches controlled certain lights because there were too many of them. I brought my label maker into work one afternoon and labelled them all during some downtime I had. It makes daily life easier around there especially when you're in a rush.

• Other than helping pass the time, another good reason to clean and organize during slow times is you'll be able to tell if you're low or missing supplies. This is important as you may still have time to order supplies before a busy event.

Look After Your Staff Room

Every Tuesday, I clean up our staff room since it's always kept locked and we don't have a cleaning person who goes in there. I empty the trash can and pick up any garbage littering the floor. Because coworkers enter for their breaks and eat food or drink while doing their cash-out, I take cleaner and wipe the table with it to get rid of any glass rings, crumbs or spilled make-up. For shoes or boots that are in the way, I put them in the old milk crate that houses the random footwear. Any clothing that litters the floor is put into an unlocked locker I labelled *lost clothing*.

If there are any reservations for the end of the week, during slow times is the time to write out any reservation signs and organize them so they're ready to go.

It's a good idea to check stock every week. You should always have an extra box or case of all the glassware you carry at the bar. When big events happen and the bar is filled to almost over capacity, you can pull out the extra stock when needed. When the event is over, all glassware is washed and put away for next time. If there seems to be a lot of breakage, you have back up, but remember to order another case right away if you get low. Organization is the key to running an efficient and busy bar smoothly.

If you have a big event planned for a night, have all your weapons ready to go before the army comes rushing in. You should have a stack of rags ready to go, extra pens sitting in a glass, extra calculators and whatever other tools are needed. All reservation signs should be out and make sure everyone is clear on their duties and sections they're responsible for. You don't want any miscommunication since there won't be any time for mistakes. We like to move any tables in high traffic areas for the servers and food runners.

Why You Should NEVER Sit Down on Shift

I've heard of servers who would grab a coffee and sit down at a table with friends or regulars when the room is slow. I knew of a server who worked in another strip bar tell me she would sit at the bar with her crossword puzzle book when she had nothing to do. This is an extreme no-no and I'll explain the reasons why.

1. You neglect the customers sitting in the room.
2. New people who walk in and sit down think there may not be a server on the floor.
3. You get too comfortable sitting down and may lose track of time.
4. It looks extremely unprofessional to everyone in the room.
5. It looks very bad to the owner or the manager if they happen to come into the room unannounced. After all, you are getting paid an hourly wage, so do something!

During slow periods, the only girl allowed to sit with customers is the shooter girl.

Whatever you do, **NEVER** sit down on a shift!

Tipping out Fellow Servers

Working at most establishments, the server keeps her tips earned but she will be expected to tip-out (share) with coworkers like bartenders, doormen, DJs, kitchen staff, bussers, and hostesses at the end of her shift. Starting at a new place, you will be told by your manager or coworkers how much will be expected for you to put aside for these people who have a hand in helping you make your tips.

I have also heard of establishments in the serving industry where all servers and bartenders throw all their tips together and then split it among themselves and everyone else.

The following information shows how to share a gratuity between several servers who had served a customer on a tab.

How to Split-up a Tip

Sometimes a customer's tab will have a few different servers who will add to his bill. This happens when a shooter girl delivers him shooters, the customer may move to another server's section or the original server goes on a break or leaves to go home. When the customer signs off and leaves a gratuity, the tip will have to be split evenly among all servers who served him.

Examples of Splitting a Gratuity

Example 1: Total of bill is $44.00. Tip left was $5.00

Mary had $19.00 worth of drinks on the bill. Sandy had $25.00 worth of drinks on the bill.
$5.00 (tip) divide by $44.00 (total amount of bill) = $0.1136
$0.1136 x $19.00 = $2.15 tip to Mary
$0.1136 x $25.00 = $2.85 tip to Sandy
If Sandy is keeping the credit card slip, she will pay Mary $21.15. ($19.00 that Mary owes for drinks at the bar and $2.15 tip).
If Mary is keeping the credit card slip, she will pay Sandy $27.85. ($25.00 that Sandy owes the bar for her drinks and the $2.85 tip).

Example 2: Total of a bill is $163.00. Tip left was $15.00

Mary had $4.00 worth of drinks. Sandy had $31.00 worth of drinks. Patty had $94.00 worth of drinks. Cindy had $34.00 worth of drinks.
$15.00 divide by $163.00 (total of bill) = $0.092
$0.092 x $4.00 = $0.37 tip to Mary
$0.092 x $31.00 = $2.85 tip to Sandy
$0.092 x $94.00 = $8.65 tip to Patty
$0.092 x $34.00 = $3.13 tip to Cindy

The server who takes over the bill has to make sure she doesn't forget to pay out the other servers, not just on the tip owed to them, but the drinks the other girls owe the bar money for. I find that forgetting to pay out a server on her drinks is quite common since everyone is so concerned with getting their portion of a tip.

Pay attention to your bills. Some may be extremely quick to work out. If I serve two beers and you serve two beers and the customer leaves a $5.00 tip, split the 5 in half = $2.50 tip each. There, done!

Share the Wealth

You don't want to rip off other servers from their tip. We're all there for the same reason and nobody likes to work for free. We all have to tip out the bartender, DJ, doorman, etc, so we are relying on that money. Don't be cheap; share the wealth. This means if a customer leaves a large tip, be honest and split it up. Don't sneak around and cheat anyone out of their portion of money. If you start ripping off servers and they find out, they'll settle all tabs in the future before they leave and you won't be trusted. You don't want this type of reputation.

One of my biggest pet peeves is if I sell a tab to another server before I go home and I find nothing in my box the next day; especially when I know of regulars who always leave me a tip. Please don't be one of these annoying coworkers where I have to grovel and ask for my gratuity! I already feel stupid asking for it once but if I have to remind you a second or third time, I am now upset. Drop it in my box in the first place. Believe me, I will not forget about it.

Same goes for bartenders and doormen. If they're done with their shift and standing there in their coat ready to go home, give them their tip without having them ask you for it.

Cleanliness

In this economy and market, it's challenging to persuade new customers to come and try out your bar, restaurant, pub, etc. Therefore, you should treat your regulars like gold since they're your bread and butter. There's a reason why they're coming into your place of work on a regular basis in the first place. I've been told the main reason why many people return to our bar frequently is because of our friendly staff who give some of the best service around.

Look at It as Your Business Too

You don't own the business, but you do work and make money there, so take pride in your room and look after it as if it were your own.

Be anal about cleanliness. When new customers decide to try out your bar for the first time, you may give great service, have big beautiful tvs (and possibly even hot dancers, if it's a strip bar) but if the place has sticky menus, dirty chairs, or garbage on the floor, it's a bad first impression and it's unlikely the customer will return. Working in a bar, the black lights highlight any white debris on the floor so pick up any tiny pieces of paper, dirty napkins, promo material, ATM receipts, bottle caps and toilet paper you notice. It's especially important during the daytime as the crowd is older and usually not drunk. Business men and women may come in for lunch with clients as well as customers who like to work on their paperwork and laptops. During the dayshift, it's rare if anyone wants to really rip it up and get drunk, unless it's some crazy people who are celebrating a birthday or a stag party early that day.

Don't neglect chairs with a sticky arm rest or spills on chair seats. Nobody wants to sit in a wet, sticky chair and get their clothes ruined.

Before handing the portable debit machine to a patron, give it a quick wipe with your damp cloth if you notice it's sticky or wet.

When picking up garbage off the table, inspect cigarette packs before removing them. If it feels light, open it and peek inside. I can't count how many times I've grabbed a cigarette pack, thinking it was empty and threw it in the trash, only to have the owner ask me if I took it. I have to dig it back out because he tells me there are joints or a cigarette hidden inside.

If your coworkers get in the habit of throwing dirty rags on the floor by the till because it's easy and fast, place a small pail there so it looks neater or hand all dirty rags to the bartender to hide behind the bar.

Don't let staff, dancers, or customers throw any food into your garbage can by the waitress till. Give it a few hours and you'll start to smell it and this makes concentrating at the till almost unbearable. Take it from someone who knows … prawn tails are brutally offensive in smell by the end of the night and you're usually gagging by the time you're ready to go home! Maybe a little more important: all servers have had to dig through the garbage at one time or another, looking for a $100 pull tab, a customer's bill or a pen that falls in by accident.

Why You Should Keep Your Section Spotless at all Times

This is another SUPER important tip to keep in mind because it will increase the tips you will end up with at the end of your shift. I have mentioned this a couple other tips in this book but I can't stress how important it is so that's why I sound like a broken record.

When customers walks in and scan the room, they'll be attracted to the cleanest looking table. Keep all chairs pushed in since it makes the room look neater and those chairs won't be in your way when you come by with a full set of drinks next time around. I've bruised my legs by kicking into chairs sitting in my way in the aisle.

When I'm working the floor with other servers, I make sure I'm even more on top of keeping my side of the room clean. The reason for this is because when new patrons walk in, they'll always steer towards a clean table positioned straight with pushed in chairs and neatly arranged promo material on it. *If all my tables are full of customers, I am maximizing my sales and tips.*

Keep the stage area clear of empty bottles and glasses. This is important since girls are dancing, kicking their legs and whipping around the pole. They can kick into glassware or bottles and this is dangerous for customers. Full drinks and jugs are kicked over at times too, but you can minimize accidents by keeping empties from stacking up at the stage.

If I notice a girl sitting on her guy's lap at the stage area, I'll let her know it's safer for her to sit in her own chair because with her sitting in someone's lap, it's easy for her to get kicked by a dancer.

Remove All Broken Furniture

As you move chairs and reorganize tables day in and night out, sometimes you'll find broken chairs or a tabletop that has popped off. Pull any broken pieces of furniture out of the room and let the maintenance man know to repair it.

Recently, I had a customer pull on his stool and he ripped his finger on a nail from under the seat. As he sat there bleeding profusely, I apologized like crazy while I ran off to get him clean napkins and bandages. Sometimes you don't notice the broken chair until it's too late but when you do, remove it from the room immediately.

My husband and I like to eat out now and then as I'm sure you do as well. Once in a while, we end up with a server who's wearing a very dirty apron. It's hard not to notice this as it hovers above our table top while the she stands there asking for our order; not appetizing! I'm sure we're not the only customers who notice this. If you wear an apron, change it every day or when it starts to look dirty and stained. Same for your top; keep a back up at work in case of accidents and spills.

Chapter 6
The Different Types of Customers

The "Regular" Customer

Regulars are the same people you see visit the bar most of the time and you get to know their name and/or what they drink.

I read a very fascinating and interesting book called *How to Win Friends and Influence People by Dale Carnegie*. This 70 year old book contains intriguing information that helps the reader understand the psychology of people and it can definitely help you deal with the public in this line of work. I highly recommend you hunt down this book and read it.

When a Regular Shows Up

If you're busy or on the opposite side of the room and you notice a regular walk in and sit down, a smile with eye contact and a quick wave works well. He knows I've seen him and I'm on the way with his drinks so this keeps him from getting up and going to the bar which means a possible tip for me. If he sits in another server's section, let that waitress know what he drinks. Your coworker will appreciate it and so will your regular.

During slow times, spend a minute or two chatting up with customers by asking how their cruise was or how their wife enjoyed the spa gift certificates you suggested when you were asked for advice on what they should get for their wife's birthday. Customers are thrilled when you remember the little things that seem so insignificant and they'll be amazed at your memory. You may even gain the position as their "favourite waitress!"

Listen to your customer's needs. If you're always being asked for a certain new beer or liquor, ask management if there's a chance they may be able to bring it in. It may end up being a hot seller which would make management happy, your customers happy and you'll be happy counting your tips!

On a regular's birthday, ask the bartender to promo them a drink. If the bar's promo tab is full, pay for it yourself. Your customer will appreciate the nice gesture. After all, these are the people who tip you on a consistent basis and buying one drink isn't going to make you bankrupt.

Memorizing Names

To memorize names, I have found myself writing the person's name down and what they drink. Then I visualize their face and keep the little cheat sheet by my till for a few hours and look at it repeatedly throughout my shift. At the end of my shift, I will pop it into my box where I will come across it a few more times in the next few days. Pretty soon, I've got the name and face memorized and this is when I throw the sheet out. I have also caught myself learning names of regulars as I compare them to people I know with the same name as theirs.

I try to learn as many regular customers' names as I can. It's important to know in not only greeting them properly but it can help when you discuss certain customers with other servers regarding tabs.

In Dale Carnegie's book he says, *"Remember that a person's name is to that person the sweetest and most important sound in the language."* Not only is it important to know their name, but to pronounce it properly and spell it correctly. In my opinion, this is one out of many important pieces of advice you will find in Dale Carnegie's book.

Throughout my life I've had people call me Ramona and it makes me cringe. Not because I dislike the name but because it's not my name. When a stranger reads my name out loud and says it correctly, I'm thrilled and touched because he cared enough to make an effort and pronounce it correctly.

Make it a game to learn as many customers' names as you can. When I'm given a credit card to start or sign off a tab, I'll look at the name on the card and use that name as often as I can.

Another way to learn customers' names is to ask the customer's friend when he leaves the room to use the restroom or to have a smoke.

Asking the other servers if they know the customer's name is another way of finding out a name.

The easiest way to learn a person's name is by simply asking them. You'd be astonished at how touched people are that you want to make the effort of remembering their name and they're thrilled when you greet them by using it on their next visit. You'll feel like an old friend and in return you may be pleasantly surprised to see your tips increase!

Humour Your Customer

Working in the service industry, you have to be ready for the wise cracks and jokes. If dumb comments make you mad or you break down crying, this job will be hard for you to deal with.

When my regular Jimmy visits the bar, he loves to joke around with me, "So Ro, when are you on stage?"

I smile and reply, "I'm on at 3:00 AM, Jimmy." The bar is closed by one in the morning and this is some fun we play between the two of us.

Coworkers in the past have admitted to me how this infuriates them when customers ask when they will be dancing on stage. I could never understand why a comment like that would bother them because it's just a guy's way of saying how he finds you attractive. Frankly, I find it quite flattering.

Turn it into a game of amusement. Sometimes guys ask me, "Why aren't you up on stage?"

I reply with, "Who's going to serve you drinks if I'm on stage getting naked? I don't want you guys to die of thirst!"

The guys love the comeback and laugh. Sometimes the game continues, "We'll wait to order a drink until you finish your show and get off stage."

I continue with, "I'm really very shy. But I do have some interesting news for you guys."

They ask, "What?"

I finish off the conversation with, "I have the exact same parts as she does!" as I point at the girl on stage, smile and walk away before they have a chance to respond. I leave them in a joking and happy mood which means I'm still in their good books to still get a tip. If you act like a grouch and get mad at them, most likely you've lost the tip.

Dealing with Death

I have come to know many wonderful people in this industry over the many years. Considering the length of time I've been there, I've known many regulars who have passed away. Some have died from heart attacks, another died from a stroke, a few have passed of a suicide, some have died from emphysema, one from a motorcycle accident and my most recent was from a boating accident.

At the time of writing this book, a regular who was my age and whom I've known for the entire time I've been working at my bar, died in a tragic boating accident. He was part of our bar family as he was friends with all the staff. He visited our bar on a daily basis since it was considered his second home.

The week of his death, we kept his usual table unoccupied and friends would buy his usual double Stoli water cranberry drink and leave it on his table. At the funeral, I was amazed at the amount of people who appeared to pay their respects as the church was jammed full and there were still at least one hundred of us stuck outside. He was loved by all and had many friends. My friend and bartender said to me, "Isn't it funny how all these people we see at the bar every night, acting like complete idiots, act like civilized human beings at a funeral." He couldn't be further from the truth. Death is usually unforeseen and is to be expected as it's a part of life. It's funny how it brings people together.

The night of the funeral, the bar was packed and again we didn't let anyone sit at Ty's table. At one point in the evening, someone had set a couple of tea lights beside the drinks and a short time later, there was a picture of him (placed in a plastic baggie) standing against one of the cocktails. Periodically I wiped up the condensation that dripped from the glasses off the table and this was the last table I cleaned up at the end of the night.

Sunday morning, Rod and I were talking about the funeral and I said, "For years, every single time Ty came into the bar, he always gave me that flirty little smile of his and he never forgot to say to me, "Romansky, you look spectacular!" Who's going to inflate my ego like that anymore?" All of the staff miss him and still wait for him to come sauntering in at any time. I was told from many of his friends they still wait for him to call them on their cell phones. It's a weird feeling. We will always miss you, dear friend.

Death is something you'll eventually have to deal with because you do get attached to people in this industry. How could you not? If you are in the service industry and enjoy it, you must love people.

Other Important Random Information

During the nightshift, the lighting is more subdued. The volume of the music is kept a little lower during the day because some customers come in to converse with friends and enjoy a lunch. Business associates are brought in to talk business and the energy level is a bit more unobtrusive as the majority of clientele is older and a more mature crowd. The times I do notice the young come in frequently during the dayshift is during spring break and summer when school is out.

If customers complain about the music being too loud or ask you to change the channel on the big screen to the World Championship Soccer Game in Scotland or the monster trucks finals, don't tell them to go tell the DJ themselves. Provide good customer service and walk over and ask the DJ yourself.

As for the temperature in the room, keep it at a moderate level. If you crank up the heat because you are cold and you notice customers sweating and complaining of the temperature, turn it down and slip on a sweater. Make the room's ambiance comfortable so your customers want to stay and enjoy themselves. Many years ago during the hot summer when our air conditioning was broken for a couple weeks, the temperature was sweltering and our room was emptying by the minute. Some of my regulars told me that even though they wanted to stay, they couldn't stand the heat any longer. I didn't blame them because I was in the washroom every half an hour dumping my black shirt under the sink in cold water and then putting it back on again.

Get to know your regulars and what they like. Every Thursday afternoon, two of my regulars order bottles of Budweiser. I know they want me to bring frosty mugs and coasters to set the pints on. They always want a menu with their drinks and to run a tab. When they enter, I pour the contents of the bottles into frosty glasses and deliver their coasters and menus. As I set it all down, I'm greeting them with, "Hi Andy and Michael! How's your day going?" I wait to hear their response and then I let them know about the lunch special. I don't ask them for money as they always run a tab separately.

A couple of other regulars always drink the pints on special. When they pay me with a twenty and some change, all change given back is in five dollar bills as this is what they like to put on the stage to tip the dancers. I will never hand over a ten dollar bill unless I ran out of fives. This is the routine with these guys and it doesn't change.

Every regular will have their specifics as well. When I see my regulars walk in and sit down, I grab their drink of choice and anything else they expect and bring it immediately.

The "Creep"

I have dealt with my share of creeps and it can be rather unnerving. I start to feel out of control because in the beginning while I'm nice and polite to this person, I'll have to turn the tables and act mean to get him off my back.

The next story I'm about to tell you about, is my "Biggest Creep" story. It upset me enough that I was contemplating on looking for another job just to get away from him.

Many years ago, I had a customer who visited the bar periodically and I saw him on my nightshift every few weeks. He barely spoke a word and was always very quiet and kept to himself.

Months went by and he started coming into the bar more frequently. I didn't think too much of it as many guys are in the bar on a regular basis. We started calling him Pineapple, because all he drank was pineapple juice. I was super nice to him and I felt sorry for him since he always visited the bar alone.

One afternoon while I was walking through the room, Pineapple was sitting in the corner of the room at a table by himself. As I walked by, he waved me over. I leaned in to hear what he had to say and to this day I remember the exact words he said to me. The hairs on the back of my neck stood up as I heard him say, "I just want to let you know that I really, really, really like you and I can't stop thinking about you."

I was stunned. I looked at him and spit back, "I'm married and have a daughter and I don't go out with customers!" I walked away and was taken aback. I made a mental note to myself that when he comes in from now on, I would bring him a drink and not lead him on with any small talk or smiles anymore.

As the weeks went by, when he would enter the bar and sit down, I would walk straight over with his pineapple juice. He would say, "Keep $.50 for yourself," and I would abruptly respond with a "Thanks" and scoot away. I was aware of my body language and conversation because I wanted him to see I was all business and not interested in him in the least.

I knew things were getting a little creepy when customers and staff commented to me, "Ro, whenever that Pineapple juice guy comes in, he stares at you all the time. Everywhere you walk in the room, he would swivel around in his chair to keep his eyes on you … even when there's a naked girl on stage!"

I quickly became aware of his presence when he entered the room. When he did, I would slip my sweater on and zip it up and then I had a hard time concentrating on my job because I started to feel uneasy and anxious. At times, I felt his eyes on me and when I would look over to see if he was staring at me, I would always meet them. Glaring back at him with a mean look, he continued to stare and he just didn't get it!

I stopped delivering his drink when he came in and I would ask another server to take it out. If I was the only server on the floor, he would eventually go to the bar and get his drink himself since I would ignore him.

One afternoon a group of guys came into the bar and as Pineapple was leaving, he stopped at the table to chat with them for a few minutes. After he left, I went over to the group and asked them if they knew him. They told me his name and that he has a wife and four children! They said they worked with him and he is absolutely harmless. I was amazed when I thought of this sucker who lay for three or four hours in a bar by himself a few times a week hitting on waitresses and stalking me!

I asked the manager at the time if we could just bar him from coming in anymore. He said, "We can't just bar him for looking at you, Ro. It's a strip club." I understood his point.

One afternoon while Pineapple was sitting there gawking away at me as I started to sweat like a hog in my sweater, I felt the anger arise in my body. I was mad at him for making my job unbearable and unpleasant. As I walked behind him, I saw him start to swivel his chair, repositioning himself to check my butt out when I would walk away. I didn't think; I reacted. I stopped behind him and dug my long fake nails into his right shoulder, then I said to him, "I'd really appreciate you stop staring at me, cause you're really making my job f-n uncomfortable! Got it!?" I walked away, dropped my tray down at the till and walked into the restroom to compose myself because I started to shake.

The next time I walked by him, he had his head bent down looking at his lap. The time after that, he was gone. He disappeared for almost three months and it was heaven! I enjoyed my job again.

One day, he started showing up at the bar again and he went back to his old ways, staring at me during my shift. I was seriously contemplating whether I should find another job, since this was really starting to upset me once more and I just couldn't put myself through this stress again. I also wondered if he would follow me to a new bar and continue his stalking.

It was getting annoying to hear people tell me, "Don't worry about it! What do you expect? You work in a strip bar. You're just another pretty girl he's checking out. He's quiet and doesn't cause any problems, so who cares!"

I CARE! And it's those quiet types you have to look-out for. I was more aware of going home at night since I didn't need this sucker following me home and knowing where I lived! My gut was telling me that this was not normal.

One evening while the bar was busy, our kitchen lady was running by Pineapple with a plate of food for another customer. Pineapple was sitting at the edge of a table and he had a habit of leaning back with his arms hugging the back of his neck. At the exact moment the kitchen lady ran by, he brought his arms down and grazed the side of her body with his left hand by accident. She started freaking out and yelling that he touched her on purpose. It was perfect timing and in his defence, I know it wasn't on purpose. The manager used this as an excuse to bar him for a month.

A month later, as I ran by the hallway from the kitchen, I noticed Pineapple standing in the hall talking to my manager. His month was up and he needed permission to start coming back into the bar. I asked a coworker to interrupt and grab my boss.

I said to him, "If you let him start coming back into the bar, I'm looking for another job. I can't work with him in the room anymore. It's too stressful on me."

He was barred for life!

It IS a Big Deal!

I often wonder what would happen if that little accident didn't happen with our food lady. Would I still be working there with him tormenting me with his stalking? I let it go way too long where it was starting to affect my job and my sanity. If this kind of thing happened again, I would approach my manager and find a way to get it dealt with and solved. I like where I work, but if nobody would be willing to help me deal with this kind of a problem, I would have to find another place to work. Fortunately, I can say that my manager and the owners wouldn't put up with this and I know for a fact they would be on my side and tell this person he's not welcome to come back.

What would you say is more important? To have happy, content staff who feel safe and enjoy coming to work or to make a few extra dollars a month for a few pineapple juices?

I don't want girls reading this book thinking that any guy who has a little crush on them can be barred or kicked out of the bar since it's not that way at all. I felt the situation was starting to get out of hand. I know guys check me out and some have a crush on me as I'm often told by their friends and get asked out frequently. This happens to most servers and I'm flattered in these cases and respond with, "Oh, that's really very sweet. I'm really flattered, but I'm married."

Most guys respond with, "He's a very lucky guy," while some will usually push a little further and ask, "Happily?"

"Yes, very happily!"

Use the Other Guys in the Room as Your Security Blanket

In the past, I have had problems with guys in regards to being hit on. Some won't take no for an answer and sometimes they get rather rude or vulgar. At this point I say, "Buddy, my husband is at the back of the room right now!" That always diffuses any other comments.

As I approach the bar, I'll tell a regular, a guy friend or one of my bad boys, "Dave, I'm using you as my husband today, so just go along with it." Many of my guys find it funny, because they know I have lots of *husbands*. Rod is grateful because I always have my big brothers looking out for me and helping me out when he's not there to do it.

Working as a server in a bar, my coworkers and I are always receiving gifts from customers, whether it's a red rose for Valentine's Day, a box of chocolates at Christmas, or a gift certificate for our birthday. It starts to get a little creepy when a server is given a box of lingerie for a gift. Yes, this has happened to others, not to me; that is the advantage of being married. I've heard of servers wearing a fake wedding ring on their finger, even if they're single to use as a diversion.

At times, guys ask me about my coworkers and whether they're single or not. It's our number one rule to say they have a boyfriend. Even if my friend is single, we all say we're taken off the market because it's easier and the girls tell me they would never date a guy who hangs out in a strip bar anyways. You may want to discuss this little rule with the servers you work with.

The Player

Some guys I wouldn't necessarily call creeps, I would call them players. The player is the guy who is always on the make. He's the guy who will ask you out for dinner, a date, or swing by with flowers or a gift.

It's kind of funny when another server comments to the rest of us about a certain customer in the room who just told her that she is extremely beautiful and he would like to take her out some time. Comparing notes, we all chime in telling each other he said the exact same thing to us as well. To this guy, it's a numbers game. He knows that by asking every girl he comes in contact with, there's always the chance one will say yes.

The Friend

I have a lot of friends and sometimes I have a very hard time making time for them in my busy schedule. This is what I tell people in the bar who want to hang out with me outside my job. I have met friends at work who are my coworkers and then I still have customers who became friends of mine who I have gone to concerts with, girls' nights out, meet at barbeques and parties or have even gone boating with. They've met my husband and some have met my daughter.

There are customers who want to weave their way into your life. You'll get invited to birthday parties and they'll give you their phone number and want you to call them up so you can go for coffee. I think you've got to be careful handing out your phone number to everyone in the bar. I'm not saying that everyone who hangs out and wants to be your friend at the bar is out to get you, you just have to be careful. Don't be naïve and think, "Oh, that guy seems so nice and sweet." That's exactly what I thought about Pineapple!

Women

When I started working in this industry over twenty years ago, the only females you would find in the strip bar were servers and dancers. Once in a while I'd notice some poor guy's wife stomp into the bar and yell at him to get his ass home or start hitting him in the parking lot because she was mad at him for hanging out in the strip bar (I've witnessed the parking lot beatings three times).

Then the movie industry came onto the scene and starting making movies like Striptease and Showgirls. Soon after, women were noticed visiting the strip bars more often.

Years ago, many of my older regulars periodically commented to me, "Ro, why are there so many women coming in here now? This is a men's club! It makes us feel uncomfortable." The strip bar used to be a gentleman's club where guys would meet their buddies after work for a beer and relax before going home. Now it's not unusual to find a couple hanging out having drinks and dinner together. I know of "swinger couples" who come in for some drinks and swap partners before leaving. Stagette parties and girlfriends like to come in and party for a few hours before taking off to go dancing at a nightclub for the rest of the evening.

The main women I deal with are staff, dancers and some female customers. Quite a few of my women regulars visit our bar and hang out with their husband, boyfriend or buddies. They're very open to the whole strip bar thing, they're easy to talk to and fun to hang around and serve. They're the girls who don't mind their man hugging you good bye and encourage him to leave you a generous tip. These are the women who comment on my perfume or the cute top I'm wearing and they're a pleasure to serve. I wish there were more of these lovely ladies.

Women customers who like to hang out in the strip bar may also be lesbian and you'll be able to tell pretty quick with most of them when they do come in as a group. Some of them will appear to dress pretty butch and have their girlfriends with them. I've had the pleasure of getting to know and serve many lesbians over the years and they're really very nice. Some of them like to hit on the servers too, so be prepared as they're no different than a male hitting on you. Take it as a compliment.

Groups of Stagette parties are fun since they interact with the dancers on the stage while they whoop it up and like to have a great time.

There's a reason why I like working in the strip bar and the majority of people I serve are men because some of the women who come in are not very pleasant. The servers and dancers often wonder why they're in the strip bar in the first place; we imagine it's to keep an eye on their guy. You'll come across the woman who doesn't want to be there in the first place and is there to either humour her man or keep an eye on him. I can usually tell within a few minutes if she'll have a problem with me since she may be rude, uptight, or seem very standoffish when ordering a drink. This is a great time to try and win her over and make a compliment about how pretty her necklace or purse is. I'll usually fish around for something to say so I can make a comment about my husband, which always seems to put her at ease and relax. If her boyfriend orders a Jack Daniels and coke, I'll say, "Exactly what my husband would order." She'll know I'm not a threat and not after her man, which in turn may help in the tip department, especially if she's the one paying the bill!

The Kids

We use the term *kids* or *babies* for young people who recently turned of legal drinking age. Doing a little research, I learned the legal drinking age is 18 in the provinces of Alberta, Manitoba, and Quebec. The rest of Canada is 19. In our bar, we encounter many young customers who cross the border and come from the

Washington State into Canada since the legal drinking age in the United States is 21.

Give the Young a Break

I know what you're thinking. You're probably groaning and thinking all young people are cheap and don't tip. You're also thinking they have an attitude problem and are more of a pain in the butt and you're hoping they don't sit in your section. Let me tell you my friend, you'd better give these young people a chance and don't make any quick assumptions about anyone.

Yes, I've had groups of young people sit on my side and not tip me a dime, but I've also had kids tip me more than generously every single time I bring them a drink that I have actually felt guilty for taking money from them.

Treat the kids with respect whether they tip or not because these patrons are your future customers who will eventually learn the art of tipping. If you're rude, you'll leave a bad taste in their mouth which would be a real shame when they learn to tip and you won't be able to benefit from it.

Clues to Look Out For in the Underage Patron

The following are some tips to look out for that may suggest your patrons might possibly be underage.

- Kids avoid eye contact with you while ordering. They look down in their lap, at the promo material on the table or at a menu.

- When ordering they say, "We'll have a jug of beer with three cups" (using the word cups, instead of glasses).

- When ordering, they say "I'll have a high ball."

They use the term high ball and when I ask them to be more specific, they don't know how to respond.

- When handing me money, they ask "Do you have change for a ten or a twenty dollar bill?"

- When you hand them their change, they automatically slip it into their pocket. Some will recount it and then slip it into their purse or pocket.

- Some people throw around their attitude while trying to intimidate you or even become defensive. They may say, "Do you have any idea who I know?!" They may even throw around another server's name like, "Is Patty working tonight? She knows who I am."

- You may have a large group of kids come in together and most of them in the group will look of age. Some servers only ID the people they think are underage, but I suggest to ID the entire group. In most cases, same age people hang out together and there may be someone in the group who forgot their ID or has an underage friend or sibling with them. In these cases, I've caught people using a friend's ID in the same group.

- Young looking girls who wear running shoes is another clue to underage patrons. Some girls are better at faking their age by dolling themselves up to try and make themselves look older. As a rule, I always ID every girl who looks under the age of thirty.

- Girls who look like they are learning to walk in high heels or look very uncomfortable in them, is another clue she may be underage.

- Usually (not always), the kids do not wear wedding rings or wedding bands.

- Most of the time (not always), the kids do not have a large amount of tattoos.

- Just because you work in the bar during the dayshift when kids should be in school, it doesn't mean they won't try coming in at this time of the day.

During the shifts when there is no doorman, I need to stay in control of my room and ID all the young people who enter the bar. This is one part of my job I dislike, but it must be done. Some kids get defensive and upset because they feel that since they've been asked for ID every single time they come in after they turn of age, you should automatically recognize them. This is when I tell them that even though I know they're of age, I'm making sure they didn't forget their ID at home. No matter what age a person is, they should always have some form of identification on themselves.

The most common line I hear is, "Don't you recognize me? I'm in here all the time!"

A friendly way to smooth over the situation is by making a comment such as, "I ID all the good looking guys!" This puts a smile on their face and the mood is lighter. You really don't want to upset them as this could affect your tip, if they happen to be good tippers.

If the person is being rude with a bad attitude, my famous line is, "Nope. You know who's in here all the time? Me. I've been here for over twenty years!"

Catching the Underage Patrons: Scenarios #1–3

Below are some examples of scenarios I occasionally deal with by staying on top of catching any underage patrons.

Scenario #1

A group of kids sit in my section, so I ask everyone to please pull out two pieces of ID. Sometimes there is one person who says he has forgotten his identification at home (I'm guessing he's underage) and I inform him he has to leave.

• There may be someone in the group who will offer you a $100 tip to let his buddy stay. As tempting as this sounds, don't do it because they may be working for the liquor control board. There may also be an under-cover liquor inspector sitting in the room or the cops or liquor inspector could do an unexpected walk-through as well. Having cops come in and do a walk-through has happened numerous times on my shift and let me tell you how unnerving this can be when you're second guessing yourself if you remembered to ID everyone.

- The person with no ID leaves the room, usually with another buddy. A few minutes later, he returns and gives you two pieces after telling you he lost it or forgot it at home. I ask everyone in the group to pull out their IDs one more time. In my experience, seven times out of ten, the ID has already been shown by someone else in the group and by asking everyone to show me their ID a second time, this is a second chance to see who in the group does not have it in the first place or passed it onto the friend.
- If you get lazy by not checking IDs regularly or never make an effort to catch the fakes, or catch the people who use another person's ID, these people will tell all their underage friends. Before you know it, you'll have tons of underage kids trying everything in the book to get into your bar. You don't want or even need the headache.

Scenario #2

When you ask someone for ID and they hand it to you, make sure you're paying attention to detail. Sometimes I'll be looking at the date and it's not sounding right in my brain until I realize the person is only 18 years old or a month shy of turning legal drinking age.

Many times I've said, "Buddy, you're only 18 years old."

The main response is usually, "Oh, I'm from Alberta."

I respond with, "Then why do you have a B.C. driver's license?" No reply. I remember when I was that age, so I don't blame them for trying since I was in the bar with my girlfriends two years before we were of legal drinking age.

Legally, a patron is to be of legal drinking age the day of their birthday, not a day before or a couple hours before midnight.

A nice way to gain a customer is by saying, "Honey, I'm sorry you can't stay, but how about you come back tomorrow when you turn 19 and I'll even buy you your first beer." If you end it on a good note, you have a happy customer willing to come back and who knows, he could end up as one of your best customers!

Scenario #3

This one is tricky and requires some memorization, especially if the group is large. I feel triumphant when I can catch these guys in their game!

When looking at a group of IDs, first check the birthday and make sure it jives with today's date. Then get in the habit of reading and memorizing the photo, as well as the first and last name. As you go through the group, you may come across the exact same person's ID (in different form such as a passport or other ID) or the person with no ID says to you he'll be right back with it because it's in the car. While you're not looking, a friend will slip him his ID that you had already looked at.

If you notice the same name or photo, don't be shy of asking everyone to pull all their IDs out of their wallets again. You'll hear groaning, so tell them what you're looking for. I'll tell the two people with the same ID to leave and inform them that if they return and pull this stunt again, I'll take the IDs away from them and hand them to the police. This keeps them from doing this another time or at least in our bar. You're just looking out for the bar's liquor license and doing your job. It's nothing personal.

The Bad Boys

The bad boys are the guys who come into the bar with loads of cash in their pocket. I'm not talking about the guy who deposits his pay cheques or flashes his money around. Don't ask the bad boys questions on what they do for a living since it's none of your business. You don't want to know anything anyways. It's safer this way.

They're usually the ones who make your night by over-tipping. They don't want any change back and these are the guys you'll bend over backwards for so keep right on top of the service! If they're having a drinking marathon, be there every spare moment you can. When one drink is half full, don't ask the one guy if he wants another drink, ask if they want another round. Nine times out of ten they'll say "yes." This is the group who will make your sales high and you'll make some enormous tips … best of both worlds!

Do yourself a favour and like I've said before, don't get involved. If you're asked by a customer where he can find blow or weed, just say you don't know. People push it a little further and say, "Oh, come on. You know! You're a waitress and all waitresses know the right people. There's some money in it for you!"

I respond with, "Sorry. I can't help you. I don't get involved with that sort of thing." Lie if you do know as the person could be an undercover cop. Just do your job and serve drinks.

You'll find you'll never have any trouble with the bad boys because they like to lay low and most don't like to bring any attention on themselves. If you do start to have any type of trouble, talk to your manager and ask what the next plan of action is. Sometimes the last resort is to call the police and get them removed out of the building. Don't get all heated and hissy with these people. You don't want to end up getting physically hurt because it's not worth it.

I heard a story on the radio a few summers about a server in a trendy restaurant having trouble with a group of guys. She got all heated with them and was yelling at them to get out of the restaurant. One guy broke a beer bottle and smashed it into her face. You never want to feel like you have that amount of power over a group of people. Don't forget that people are drinking and some are doing drugs, some are "nuts" in the first place and some just don't accept a woman yelling at them and telling them what to do, especially in front of their boys. With all the problems associated with gangs and fighting, be more conscious of your safety. If you must, call the police.

The Rude Customer

Of all the customers I have to deal with on a daily basis, the rude customer is the personality who sucks the life and energy out of me. I can handle bitchy women, the drunks, crazy party animals and the guys who constantly hit on me, but it's the dark entities who steal my positive energy and tire me out. They cause me to become snippy towards other customers, which end up affecting my tips.

These people seem unhappy with their lives and themselves. They have a bitter attitude towards others. They're disconnected from the regular folks and when you come face to face with them, you can feel the negative energy seep out of them almost immediately. They don't smile, their appearance is stiff and they stare straight ahead with piercing eyes. When they talk, it's almost with attitude as if you're annoying them with unnecessary questions, like asking what drink they'd like to order.

Same Scenario; Two Different Types of People

Scenario #1

Me — "Hi! How are you tonight?"
Him — "I'll get a Budweiser."
Me — "I didn't ask what you wanted. I asked how you're doing tonight!" I'm smiling and saying this in a joking and light- hearted way.
Him — "Oh, I'm sorry! I'm doing great. How are you? I'll get a Budweiser please." He smiles and looks embarrassed.

This person isn't rude; he must've been on auto pilot and the only thing that seems to be on his mind at the moment is beer.

Scenario #2

Me — "Hi! How are you tonight?"
Him — "I'll get a Budweiser."
Me — "I didn't ask what you wanted. I asked how you're doing tonight!" I'm smiling and saying this in a joking and light- hearted way.
Him — He'll glare at me and repeat, "I'll get a Budweiser."

I'm sure he's thinking I'm a smart ass, but that's okay because I'll walk away and get his beer. I'll also make a point of neglecting him for the rest of the night because I don't need people to treat me like dirt. If he tries flagging me down for a second beer, I'll look right through him as if I don't see him and this ensures he has to get up out of his comfy chair and go stand in line for beer for the rest of the night. If he doesn't have common courtesy and good manners to not snap at someone who is there to serve him, he deserves to get it himself. I don't need his sale and tip that bad.

The Demanding Customer

The other type of rude customer you may encounter is the guy who is rather demanding.

Me — "Hi, How are you tonight?"
Him — "I'll get a pint," he commands as he raises his eyebrows and many times I've even had him snap his fingers at me.
Me- — "Sure. And the magic word is?" I'll mirror him by raising my own eyebrows and snapping my fingers, and then I stop and smile sweetly.

As a result, I've evened the score so he knows I'm not someone to intimidate. If he leaves me a tip, I'll dismiss it and keep the drinks coming but I won't spend much time doing small talk with him or joke around. At this point, it's all business.

The "No Manners" Customer

If it's one thing that makes a server cringe, it's the guy who yells, "Hey!" to get my attention.

Depending on how busy I am, I ignore him and keep walking or I respond with, "Hay is for horses and kinky women! I don't respond to hey!" Usually the person apologizes and I'll respond with, "That's ok, I'll forgive you," to lighten the mood.

I couldn't believe my ears one night when a young punk said, "Well, what am I supposed to call you?"

I retorted with, "Well, excuse me works. Or even waitress. Or how about my name, it's Romana!" He was lucky I even responded to his rudeness because when I'm busy I won't even stop and waste my time explaining to people how disrespecting that sounds.

The Jerk

From time to time I have creeps say to me, "Shit, you got nice tits!"

When the other servers and I talk about why a guy would make this comment, we all wonder what's going through his head. Does he wonder we think, "Oh good! I'm glad he told me because I wasn't too sure if they were nice or not."

There are a couple of different ways I've handled these guys. If the guy says it basically with his tongue drooling and acting like a pig, I like to respond with, "You know what? I'm someone's wife and mother! I don't think my husband would appreciate you talking to me like that." I'll usually get an apology and the guy always looks around as if to find a huge bodybuilder standing behind him, ready to grab him by the neck. I get a kick out of it as I watch him squirm in his chair.

If the guy says it matter of fact, I say "My husband thinks so too!" and I walk away before he has a chance to respond or even order a drink.

I know of servers who have asked the guy, "Do you have a wife or girlfriend?"

If the guy responds with "yes" The server says, "I wonder why!" If he responds with "no" She says, "I'm not surprised!"

You have to have a sense of humour in this industry. If you know this would grate on your nerves and you couldn't handle it, maybe this isn't the type of place for you to work.

It took me a few years to grow a thick skin and stop coming home at the end of my shift in tears because I've learned to just deal with it and take things as they come. When I leave work after a shift, I leave it all behind and don't dwell on it. I like to entertain

Rod with stories about the crazy people I dealt with that day and leave it at that.

A regular asked me once how much I make in tips on a regular basis. I responded with, "Well Bob. If I give you a small number, you're going to think I'm an idiot for putting up with all this. If I tell you a big number, you're going to stop tipping me!" He loved my response.

Many times customers ask me if I make good money. I tell them it's the only reason why I work where I do. They say, "Good. You deserve it, because to deal with some of these people on a daily basis, I don't know how a woman handles it." I'm glad someone notices!

The High Maintenance Customer

You'll encounter the guy who thinks everyone is against him or he's not getting his money's worth. These are the people who don't stop and think before they yell at the server as they imagine that everything is our fault.

"Hey! When the hell is there another stripper on? I've been sitting here paying close to six bucks for a beer and I've only seen one peeler! What the hell is going on around here?"

To this person I respond with, "Excuse me, but I do not respond to hey. And just so you know, the dancer called in saying she'll be late so it throws off our entire schedule. We're doing our best in getting another girl to take her show."

"Hey, why is it so cold in this room? Can't you guys afford to turn the heat on?"

"Why are you guys showing motorcycle stunts on the big screen? Why don't you change the channel to the golf championships?"

"Why do the fries have salt on them?"

This customer will always seem to find something to whine about. Do your best to try and win over the situation because you do want to make him happy and in the end, you still want to make a tip.

For example, if the room is cold, tell him you'll turn the heat up. If he doesn't like the motorcycle stunting show, tell him you'll ask the DJ to turn the channel to the golf championships on the

TV set close to him. If the fries are too salty, tell him you'll ask the cook to make him a new batch with no salt on them. Sometimes you have to grit your teeth and make the customer happy, no matter how annoying and demanding they may seem.

In this business, the customer is not always right as you've been taught to believe. People don't have the right to come into your place of work and treat you like their slave. You don't deserve to be yelled at, have them demand things from you or disrespect you. Of course you don't want to be unprofessional and scream back at them, but you want to be firm, keep the upper hand and stay in control. If I can't seem to smooth over a situation and end up with more problems with the complainer, I'll get the manager (if he's in) or ignore him for the rest of the night. If the customer is so rude to the point of upsetting me and getting me close to tears, I'll end up getting the doorman or DJ to ask him to leave.

The Drunk

It's illegal and looks bad for the bar when customers see someone stumbling around in the bar and they're still being served alcohol. While you're worried about their safety, there could also be a chance a liquor inspector might show up unexpectedly. The more a customer drinks (especially at a fast pace), he becomes intoxicated and as a result, must be cut off.

There are many reasons why a person can get intoxicated much more quickly than the average drinker. Some reasons are:

He drinks while on an empty stomach

The person is mixing alcohol and illegal or legal drugs

The customer is drinking doubles in short glasses or consuming martinis, which automatically contain two ounces of alcohol, at a fast pace

He's drinking large amounts of shooters while drinking a beer or cocktail

He started his drinking binge at home or another bar prior

Keep in mind, a drunken person walking will be easier to recognize than the drunken person sitting at a table. Indications pointing at the customer who's in a drunken state are slurred, mumbled, or loud speech, or even opposite: fast talking. Coordination isn't present, such as trouble picking up change off the table. Eyes may be half closed, glassy, bloodshot, blank stare that is staring at nothing in particular, nodding off as if falling asleep and may jerk his head back up suddenly. The complexion may be beet red in color and as he sits in his chair, he may sway side to side and not sit still. Throwing up at the table is a big sign as he is usually too drunk to make it to the restroom. As he walks, he may weave, stumble, or shuffle and even walk into a table, chair or another person. As he walks with a drink in his hand, it may spill all over his hand because he can't seem to keep his hand steady.

Ethically, it's really bad judgment for staff to continue serving a person in an intoxicated state because of the fact he keeps over-tipping. I've seen it on more than one occasion.

Some servers are worried they'll make the wrong decision by thinking the customer isn't that drunk yet. If you even have a small suspicion, cut him off sooner rather than later. Later could end up being too late. Besides, even if you're wrong in your decision, all staff members must honour and stand behind you.

Once in a while, a customer who enters your bar is possibly mentally handicapped or has some other disability which makes him seem slower. Sometimes these people will usually visit the bar with a friend or family member who will let you know of their state should you have any concerns.

Be especially aware in summer weather. I find a lot of people spend the day in the sun and love to finish off their partying in the bar. They're out drinking and sitting in the sun all day which can be very dehydrating to their system.

Stand Behind Your Coworkers

Years ago, we used to have a bartender who would still serve customers when I told him they were cut off. It makes me look like I don't know what I'm doing when staff goes against my decision. In the end, the person ends up becoming more of a problem while they get more intoxicated and I'm always the one to have those famous last words with that bartender, "I told you so!!"

I'll let the drunk know he is cut off, as well as all staff from the bartender, DJ, doorman, and all servers, to the shooter girl. If the person is drinking solo, it's up to the server serving him to make sure he has a safe ride home. Offer to call the person a cab or ask them if they need a phone to call someone for a ride. We have a company which can be called and they arrive to pick up the intoxicated patron and their vehicle and can deliver them both home safely.

Watch out for large groups such as stag parties. It seems like these people want their friend to get so inebriated that can't stand. So, to cut off that person without cutting off the group will be trouble. I have found in the past that if the whole group is not cut off unless the drunk is taken home, they'll continue sneaking alcohol to him. Pretty soon, they need to carry him out or he ends up puking all over the place and it's not a pretty scene.

My regulars have a lot of respect for me, so if someone is to be cut off, I let the friends of the drunk know. They honour that and the only person who seems to have a problem with being cut-off is the person himself.

If a customer is overly intoxicated, according to the law, he must be sent home. But if I have a regular who is not that drunk to be sent home yet and he's with friends looking after him, I'll keep him happy by serving him pretend drinks.

I have found a way to make everyone happy. Read to find out how.

The Strategy of Serving the Drunk "Pretend" Drinks

If a customer ends up being "cut off" and you give him non-alcoholic drinks for the rest of his visit by pretending they contain alcohol, there are some good reasons for this.

1. It keeps the drunk from getting drunker.

2. It keeps the peace with the drunk because he won't be arguing with you as to why he is being cut off. He's quiet and kept happy and he thinks he's still drinking with the group.
3. You want this group to stay if the rest of them is not a problem.
4. By letting the group stay and continue having fun, you have happy customers who will return. If you kick out the drunken patron, usually the rest of the group will leave too.

Do not charge the intoxicated person for the drink if it's a virgin drink because it's only some juice and ice. If he tries paying for it, tell him it's been looked after by someone already. You're making money off his friends, so giving some virgin drinks away isn't a big deal. Usually a friend in the group will pay for the non-alcoholic beer, if a "beer" was ordered by the drunk.

If the drunk complains the O'Doul's/mocktail tastes funny (of course it does since it contains no alcohol!) and they want something else, take the drink back to the bar and top it up with more juice or pour the beer into a fresh frosty pint and return it to the customer. Generally, about 99 percent of the time, he won't complain anyways because he's too drunk to even notice or care. When giving the virgin drinks to a person who is cut off, let other servers and even the manager know, so in case the liquor inspector or police show up, everyone knows what is going on.

Serving a drunken customer is a fine line. By law, the drunk needs to be cut off immediately and the server must make sure he gets home safely.

If the customer is really drunk and management or the liquor inspector find out you're allowing this person to stay and you're still serving him (even if the drinks are non-alcoholic), you could get yourself into trouble. Also, if customers see you serving the drunk (and not knowing the drinks are non-alcoholic), they may complain to management and you'll look like you don't know how to do your job.

*It is a **very rare circumstance** where I allow the drunk to stay and serve him non-alcoholic drinks.*

If you're unsure what to do or you are new to this line of work, always ask someone of authority. To stay on the safe side, just cut the customer off and send them home.*

When You Should Ask a Customer to Leave

I cut off a whole group of heavy drinkers when I have a feeling trouble is starting to brew or the drunk is wandering around not seeing straight. If they're all getting out of hand, they're being loud or rude, or other customers are starting to complain in the room, then I want them all to leave. This is the time when I let them know everyone in their party is done and will no longer be served. It's better to get rid of a group like this as soon as you can because they can start to unnerve your other customers and cause others to leave. You don't want the trouble makers to stay because this is when a fight can break out.

If a customer throws up, is way too drunk, is falling asleep in their chair or is ready to fight, it's time for them to go anyways.

Chapter 7
The Cocktail Waitress Tray and Money

Holding, Arranging and Balancing Your Tray

If you've never held a tray and tried balancing it on your arm, it may take you a bit of practice. Before you know it, you'll be handling it like an old pro and whizzing around the room.

These are the instructions for a right-handed person. If you're left-handed, reverse them.

Place all your paper money into your left hand. When you're ready to take your tray, start to slide it off the counter with both hands. When half of it is off, steady it while you slip your left hand underneath and then with your right hand, continue to slide the rest of the tray off onto your left hand and forearm smoothly as not to spill or tip any drinks; fingers are spread apart to take as much surface of the tray in your hand. Take the weight of it and lay it onto your forearm, moving your hand a little to the left or the right to balance it. Keep your right hand on the edge of the tray until you have it steady and the tray is balanced securely on your left arm.

As your tray sits on your forearm, you'll want your coin holder (cash caddy or ashtray) positioned on your tray where it's located closest to your body, which should be your left boob (I heard a few giggles). This is for the safety of your money and the convenience of reaching for change. You don't want your coin on the other end of the tray where you have to reach for it around tippy Corona bottles and risk dropping change into customer's drinks.

You'll know when you're holding all the weight of your tray on your wrist if it's cocked at an upward angle and singing with pain after a couple of hours. You want to feel the weight pull down on your shoulder and be supported on your forearm.

The first few years of serving, I started sporting a wrist brace after the suggestion from one of my coworkers. She wore one because her wrist ached with pain and discomfort while working. I was embarrassed wearing it because it looked ugly and eventually started to look dirty and discoloured but I had no choice since I was in too much pain.

I guess I started holding the load of my tray on my forearm and let my shoulder take the weight to compensate for the pain I was having in my wrist. Before I knew it, the discomfort disappeared and I rationalized about how I started carrying the weight differently. I came upon it on my own, by accident. As you start to work with your tray in this manner, you'll find after a couple of hours, muscles in your shoulder, arm and back you never knew you had will start to throb or tighten with pain. It'll take you a while to build up strength in those muscles, but before you know it, you'll have people commenting on your pipes (biceps). Don't be surprised when random guys will challenge you to an arm wrestle! My response is always, "No, I better not. I don't want to embarrass you in front of your friends!"

You may remember seeing cocktail waitresses in nightclubs or in the movies holding their tray high above their head. I can understand why girls will heave their tray high up in the air and meander through the room to deliver drinks safely to their customers, but I wouldn't recommend it or do it myself. I'll give you some reasons why:

- I make it a point to stop often and quickly while grabbing an empty or leaning in to hear a soft-spoken person give me their drink order. I wouldn't want to keep heaving my tray up and down so I could rearrange and place empties on it.

- Someone may bump into me, throw my tray off balance and knock it to the ground, where I would end up paying for the drinks lost.

- I may get knocked into by someone and spill my tray onto a customer; they could get very hurt, not to mention it would soak and ruin their clothing. Accidents like this may result in a bar fight among guys.

- A drunk who's trying to be funny may reach over and tickle your armpit.

- You could eventually wear out your shoulder from the weight and rotating of balancing heavy loads while you move your tray up and down constantly.

- In a very busy bar, you don't have your eyes on your tray as it is high up in the air. Tall guys could reach up and try to steal a drink and this would upset your tray balance, knocking it out of your hand.

As you move around the room, be conscious of your surroundings and hold your right arm out like a blocker if the bar is very busy. If someone were to stand up or step back towards me, I have my arm out to protect my tray so they don't knock into it.

Use your voice as often as you can because it's a very powerful tool! While walking through a crowd of people, talk in a firm, loud voice so customers know you're right beside or behind them, "Excuse me! Excuse me please! Excuse me guys!" If you speak low, customers won't hear you. Always remember you're constantly competing for them to hear you above the loud music, friends conversing and everything else. If your right hand is free, touch them firmly on the back or arm as you pass by.

Watch the speed of your walk while matching it to the activity and energy level in the room. If the energy is low and the room is not busy while you're working the dayshift, slow down. I'm not saying to dawdle, but do walk with a purpose. If you're delivering to two guys at opposite sides of the room, walk straight over to them and never mind keeping to the map of your room. Deliver those drinks first and then walk around the rest of the room, keeping care not to neglect any customers.

If you've got a lot of orders to take out because the room is full of patrons and buzzing with energy, pick up your speed, and walk briskly while making sharper and quicker motions. You'll need to start multi-tasking by reaching for empty bottles two at a time and asking customers to hand you any empties you can't reach. You'll have your neck craned while listening to customers giving you their drink orders while at the same time you're rearranging empties and drinks on your tray, collecting money from another customer or collecting empties from the next table. This is when you'll want to stay on the map of your room because it ensures you get to everyone and nobody is neglected.

Be Aware of the Helpful Customer

It's very sweet when a customer wants to help you by putting empties on your tray, grabbing your rag off your ashtray to mop up a spill or remove drinks. The only problem is that this move will unbalance your tray and it'll spill all the contents in his lap. Grab his hand quickly before he's had a chance to unbalance it and stop him in his tracks. You have to be fast and firm and say, "Thanks for trying to help, but when you grab my beer/rag/whatever off my tray, you unbalance it and it'll tip off my arm and all the drinks and empties will land in your lap!" People don't think and when you explain this to them, it computes in their head as not to touch your tray.

These people also reach over and drop coin onto your tray or into your coin holder. Coin has been dropped into a full beer or can bounce into a drink if they drop it on your tray or it could land on the floor. If you hear them say, "Hold on!" and they're rooting around for a tip for you, hold out your hand before they have a chance to dump it on your tray.

Unloading Your Tray

You end up at the bar with a full tray of empties. Full tray in, full tray out, right?

Put the edge of your tray onto the counter smoothly and slide it so the whole thing sits on the surface. Don't leave half your tray sitting off the edge because as you unload it, it could tip off the counter, spilling all your change and anything that's left on your tray to the floor. Yes, this has happened to me twice and it sucks crawling around on the floor in the dark while you hunt for loonies and quarters that lay in stale beer spilled on the dirty floor. You wonder if you lost any money as coins could roll under the counter or fall into the trash can.

Drop any visa slips into your waitress box. This is also the time I drop any large bills after I do a second inspection of them and make sure they're real. All money type stuff is dealt with first.

Do you ring in your order before you forget any of your drinks or unload your tray of empties first? Our waitress area is very small, so if I'm working a nightshift with other servers whom I have to share the space and till with, I'll unload my tray first as to be out of the way of the next girl who comes up with a full tray of empties. As I'm unloading my tray, I'll start to think of my drinks I need to ring in and organize them in my head. Then I start punching in my drinks into the till after I move my tray out of the way towards the bartender. If I leave my full tray in the way while I start punching in an order, the next girl who comes up with a full tray of empties will have nowhere to put it.

Working by myself on the dayshift, I ring in all my drinks and any food items first so nothing is forgotten. This way, the bartender can get busy and start getting everything I need onto the counter. I take a quick look around the room to make sure I haven't forgotten anyone. This is when I may end up punching in the remainder of any other drinks.

Unload your tray and place all empty bottles in their proper case. If you fill a case, dispose of it immediately so you don't leave it for another server. Empty any ice and straws from dirty glasses into the sink, and then place the glass upside down on the glass washer. Turn on the glass washer if it's near full. Any garbage collected at tables is thrown into the trash can and not into the sink. If you have a spare moment, run hot water into the sink to melt any ice and make more room. Dirty straws left in the sink after the ice has melted are thrown into the garbage. Give your tray a quick wipe if it has any spills on it before reloading with the next load of drinks.

Take a peek at your change inventory. Do you have only two quarters left and need to buy another roll from the bartender? I always like to have plenty of fives, tens, and twenties on hand for change. People may pay you in fifties and hundreds, while others will ask to buy a bunch of five dollar bills so they can tip the dancers on stage so sometimes I run low on small bills. I hate when I need to run back to the bar to buy change because it's such a big time and energy waster.

If you need to run back to the bar in a hurry, take your tray with you!! Don't set it down and leave it behind at a table with customers. I hear horror stories of people getting drugged by having someone slip something in their drink. Keep an eye on your tray at all times. If I was a customer and I saw my drink on a server's tray and watched her leave it at a table full of random people as she ran to the bar for a forgotten drink or to buy change, I would be slightly unnerved by taking that drink afterward. Customers aren't stupid; many eyes are on you, so think before you make a move like that.

Ok, your tray is empty and your bartender is starting on your order…

Arranging Your Tray

When I started at the bar over twenty years ago, there were two round plastic trays lined with cork which kept drinks from slipping on the surface. I trained with these trays and since I've used them all these years and they're the only trays I've ever worked with, they're like a second skin. Unfortunately, the trays are only fourteen inches across. They're extremely lightweight and the outer lip stands straight up, being a bit taller than the lip on the standard sixteen- inch, heavier tray. I'll use the sixteen-inch tray when I'm slammed and when I can't seem to carry everything out on the fourteen-inch tray.

My fourteen-inch tray holds my ashtray full of coin and, if packed tightly, holds sixteen bottles of beer.

Ok, so let's say you're not overly busy and your order calls for two Kokanees, four Canadians, two Coronas, rye coke, rye diet, Bombay tonic and one jug of beer. I have a system to arrange my drinks on my tray to get full use of the space, while keeping space empty to load any empty bottles I collect. Bottles are the tallest and skinniest, so I like to arrange them all on the left side, tucked tightly together against my ashtray. To save time, arrange the bottles so you can read their labels at a glace and you can retrieve the ones wanted without hunting and turning them around to find the right brand.

I remember the first time a drink order contained ALL bottles. I stacked them tightly against one another and I had to take off the ashtray and put it aside since I had no room for it. I dumped some coin around the bottom of the tray for change to hand back to customers. I made it to the first table while my arm shook the whole time from the weight and as I looked at my tray, all I saw were brown bottles! I had to hunt through all the bottles picking them up and turning them around looking for the right brand the customer ordered. (Don't forget I don't put my tray down on a table. It stays glued to my arm until I get back to the bar with a tray full of empties.) I learned pretty quickly to arrange them on my tray with the labels facing me!

So, the bottles are arranged on the left with labels facing you. When you remove a full bottle and replace the spot with an empty, turn the empty around so you can't see the label. This will signify an empty bottle. I love this time saver, since I don't have to pick up any empties on my tray and think they're a full beer!

I place any Corona bottles more towards the middle and let other bottles hug them. Corona bottles are easy to tip over since they are tall and skinny and as you walk with a bit of a bounce in your step, they are much easier to upset, especially with a big hunk of lime set in the opening of it.

I'll put two straws into my rye with the diet coke, one straw into the rye coke. A lime twist goes into the Bombay tonic and I make sure to put frosty mugs on the tray for the jug drinkers. I'll carry the jug in my right hand if I don't have room on my tray and I arrange my cocktails around the outside of the tray as most are in short glasses. This way it's easier to grab hold of a drink without knocking over taller drinks like bottles or Caesars.

My favourite orders are when I have customers drinking lots of bottles in the room. All of the same bottles would be arranged together starting on the left side of my tray, unless I know one of my first delivery stops will be eight Budweisers. In this case, I'll arrange everything else starting on the left side of my tray and make sure I keep those eight Budweisers more to the right, crammed against all the other bottles which are arranged on the left. Any system works, as long as it's easy and efficient for you.

If the only way you can remember a mixed drink on your tray is by putting four straws in it, then do it. Just make sure you remove three of the straws from the drink when you hand the drink to the customer. I like to put a straw in a pint of beer if something unusual were in it like 7-Up (this is referred to as a Shandy).

As you gain more experience serving, you'll find different methods work best for you. Use the alphabetical-order system if you have many mixed drinks on your tray that all look the same. A few other ways to tell drinks apart from one another are by putting two straws in all the diet pop drinks and lime twists into the vodka drinks, while the rum drinks have the lime twist sitting on the edge of the glass. Be nosy and ask senior servers why they arrange their tray the way they do and how they can tell their drinks apart from each other. You may love their system and end up adopting it. Serving is a trial and error type of a job. What may work for another server, may not work for you.

Cash Caddy vs. Ashtray

Years ago, the bars were full of smokers and over the years, laws were passed and smoking rooms were built. Today in British Columbia businesses, smoking indoors is no longer legal and smokers are forced to move their smoking habit outdoors.

During the days of customers smoking indoors, servers had to carry a small stack of plastic ashtrays on their tray and exchange the dirty ones for clean ones. We kept our coin in the top ashtray while the clean stack housed underneath was replaced with a dirty when needed. Now that we no longer require ashtrays for customers, we still use the ashtray as our coin holder out of sheer habit.

I ordered a cash caddy and now work with it for the past five years just to try something new and try as an experiment for the purpose of my book. I'd like to give you my perspectives of using both the ashtray and the cash caddy. Depending on your place of work, you might have to go straight to using a cash caddy as most bars have probably gotten rid of all ashtrays by now anyways.

Advantages of the Cash Caddy

I know servers who love their cash caddy. I love the fact you can customize them by putting your name, stickers, sparkles and decorations on it and girls can't mix up their trays amongst one another.

If you like keeping your coin organized, cash caddies are great tools. You can carry a lighter or a lipstick in there too. When the lid is flipped open, there's a pocket-like area on the underside of the lid to cram bills, credit card slips and credit cards to run your tabs. Close the lid and no one can see your money. There's a little clip on the side so you can snap the case shut and once the case is closed, there's a big handy clip on the top. A notepad or loose bills can be clipped under it, so they don't fly off your tray while you're cruising around the room. At the end of your shift, if the paper bills are neatly stacked in the cash caddy, all you need to do is pull them out and count them, which makes your cash-out very quick.

Advantages of the Ashtray

This is my preference when I work a crazy busy shift. I stack three on top of each other since this is the height I like. The ashtray doesn't take up too much space so I can cram all my drinks up against and around it.

I don't mind messy change because when I'm busy, my emphasis is on selling. I throw it in one big mess because it'll eventually get pulled out, only to be thrown back in again. I can see into my change at all times, so I know when I'm low on loonies or quarters and when I need to buy a roll. I keep a wet rag folded neatly on top of my change to keep it covered.

My bills are folded lengthwise and carried in between my fingers. It feels uncomfortable in the beginning when you're not used to it, but you'll get the hang of it pretty quick. Get in the habit of not removing it from your fingers and laying it on the counter. You could forget it and walk away. I can't count the amount of times new girls have removed their bills from their fingers to do something and then walk away. DO EVERYTHING with those bills in your hand, from punching your order into the till, unloading empties and garbage from your tray, writing up bills and even using the restroom. I take the bills out of my fingers to wash my hands only if there's no one in the restroom. If there are girls there, I do my best washing my hands with the bills intact. I'd rather have wet bills than no bills.

Disadvantages of the Cash Caddy

The cash caddy is a great little tool to have, but I found there are a few disadvantages to using it.

I found the cash caddy took up a little more room than the ashtray and I was not able to load up my tray with as many drinks as when I used the ashtray. I also now had my wet rag wasting space by sitting beside the cash caddy on the tray.

I found it virtually impossible to write on the pad because the clip is so big and got in the way. I don't write any orders down but wanted to try for the sake of this experiment. A coworker removed the big clip and uses an elastic band to hold down her notepapers.

I found that because I use my favourite fourteen-inch tray, the lip is too tall and the cash caddy won't clip to the edge unless I raise it by stacking a small pile of coasters underneath.

When I opened up the lid on the cash caddy, the big clip on the lid would hit my bottles and I'd either have to rearrange or remove them when I would need to get inside it for change. If I didn't move the bottles, they would get tipped over because of the awkward clip. I learned pretty quickly to open my lid while I loaded my tray. This would make a gap where I would not place any bottles/drinks, which I found was a waste of space. It also put more emphasis on the weight being at the outer edges and this would throw my tray balance off kilter and hurt my wrist. I didn't like the fact that customers standing around me at the bar could see inside the cash caddy when I had it open to load my tray.

I found it extremely frustrating when I needed to open the caddy to give someone change and the clip hindered me from doing so because of empties I stacked behind it. This was definitely the main thing that drove me insane, not being able to open up the caddy when my tray was full. When I was crazy busy and using the sixteen-inch larger tray, balancing bottles and drinks on the outer edge were a killer on my arm. When it's loaded to the hilt with the balance being uneven, it's extremely tiring for your arm, as well as the muscles in your back and shoulder.

By having all my bills in the cash caddy, I found myself being extremely nervous about leaving my tray on the counter (even when I did clip it shut) as I ran off to grab an order from the kitchen. The bartender can leave the bar to go get beer or ice and no one would notice if someone unclipped my cash caddy and ran out the door with it. Your tray is your responsibility, not your bartender's. At times when I would run off to the restroom, I unclipped the caddy and took it with me, which was unnerving for me while I didn't want it to fall into the toilet if I set it on the back. If I set it on the floor by my feet, I was scared someone would reach underneath the door, grab it and run out the door while I was in mid-pee.

At times when I was at the bar getting drinks, I didn't notice the change in my cash caddy being low unless I opened it to load my tray of drinks if there were many. Therefore, unnecessary trips were made by running back to the bar to buy a roll of coin.

If your shift is long or very busy, you'll still need the use of a waitress box or even an apron, as the cash caddy is not big enough to hold large amounts of money, visa slips and interac slips.

Disadvantages of the Ashtray

The biggest disadvantage I've found was if servers are using the same style of tray and also have messy coin, you or another girl can accidentally grab the wrong tray. This has happened to me a few times. As I look into the ashtray, I notice there are only three loonies and panic rises since I realize that three minutes earlier I had bought a roll. I look across the room and see the other server is delivering drinks with my tray and digging into my ashtray for change to hand to her customers.

How to Correctly Hold Your Paper Money in Your Fingers

I like to hold my paper money in my left hand, with the bills folded lengthwise all the same side folded, one on top of the other. This is the same hand and forearm that will be supporting my tray. Keep the folded parts of the bills touching the inside of the skin between the fingers. If I keep the open ends of the money against my skin, it feels sharp and feels like it will cut into my hand. I am also not able to straighten out the bill easily for the customer with the other hand.

My right hand is free to do all my other waitress duties such as using the till, grabbing empties, taking and giving money and removing drinks from my tray.

How to Be a Cocktail Waitress and Make Big Tips

I like to slip all my five dollar bills around my middle finger. My twenties are slipped around my index (wedding ring) finger, with the tens on the outside. The "fan" of money will stand up from the back of your hand.

The Goal is To Retrieve and Put Back Money Without Looking

At home, grab a large plate or serving platter and practice memorizing where your money is. Pretend your tray is full and with your hand firmly planted under the bottom of your tray, you need to pull out bills from your hand without looking. Keep your tray steady and straight as you reach under with your right hand and pull out four twenties (pretend you're giving back change for a hundred). Now you need to pull out a ten and a five. Pull your money out of your fingers slowly. If you pull too quickly, you'll remove other bills without knowing and they could fall to the floor.

When you seem pretty good at it, take it to the next level and practice this while balancing drinks on the tray.

Hand over any bills to your customer, flattened (not folded). This way he'll be able to see the bill's denomination and there's no mistake by you giving him a bigger or smaller bill.

As you pull your first bill out from your left hand, pinch it together tightly and roll your fingers across, separating the two halves and straightening it flat. It helps if you pinch your wet rag on the tray to moisten your fingers before you attempt this. The bill will stick better to your fingers and then slide apart.

Now, as you move through the room, practice folding twenties, tens, and fives and place them back into your fingers. Practice folding, unfolding and playing with your paper money.

Take it a step further and practice by putting drinks on your tray. Balance drinks and play with your money by retrieving it and placing it back into your fingers.

Inspecting Bills for Fakes

Playing with your money has its benefits. You'll be able to feel anything unusual about it and may spot a fake bill by feel. For anything that looks or feels unusual, take it up to the bar where there's more light and inspect its color, markings and size. If you're unsure, ask a fellow server or bartender for a second opinion.

Black light is your friend. Sure, it shows up bleach streaks on clothing and lint on black, but quick inspection of a paper bill, Canadian Citizenship card or a driver's license under it can detect a fake. There are holograms and marks which attest to the authenticity. During down time, pull out paper money and all sorts of identification and inspect it under the black light so you get familiar with them and know what you're looking for.

I'll always do a quick once over on a big bill when the customer hands it to me. If it looks funny or unusual, I'll hand it back to him and tell him I can't accept it. If the customer gets upset, show and tell him why you won't take it.

If you notice the color on the bill seems smudged, wet your finger on your wet rag and rub it on the bill. If the color starts to run, it's a fake and the customer is right there watching as your witness.

If the bill looks okay but feels funny, I'll tell the customer I need to inspect it some more at the bar under the lights and if there's a problem, I'll be back for a replacement bill. Do not be embarrassed. It's your money and you're responsible for it.

At the bar, I compare the bill to others under the light and even ask other staff members for a second opinion. Then I put part of the bill under running water. If the color doesn't run, the bill is good.

Since I only deal with Canadian money, the information I give you will be about Canadian currency.

Five dollar bills are light blue in color, tens are purple, twenties are green, fifties are red and hundreds are brown. Inspect all bills carefully and get familiar with them.

Front

The front has the face of the Queen or a Prime Minister. The bill will have a stripe of silver that looks hologram-like on the left running vertically. The stripe has maple leaves and the amount of the bill alternating. If you hold the bill up into the light, you'll see an invisible face close to the middle of the bill. Rub your finger nail across the lapel of the Queen or Prime Minister on the bill. It will be raised and feel bumpy. On the top right-hand side you'll feel little unusual bumps, which are brail for the blind.

Take the bill in your hand. Put your pointer finger on the back side of the bill behind the lapel, clamp the edge of the front of the bill with your middle finger, and pinch your pointer finger with your thumb. Press your finger down with the bill trapped between a piece of white paper and finger and scrub it quickly. If a line of color is left on the paper, the bill is real.

Back

Each denomination has its own scene on the back. There will be a broken stripe running vertically on the left side of the bill in a greenish-gold type hologram. On the left and right side of the bill there is a serial number. The left side will match the right side.

Are Bills That Are Torn or Have Missing Pieces Legal?

• If a customer gives you a ripped bill in half, inspect both sides of the bill's serial number. If the numbers/letters don't match, it is considered not useable.

• If a bill has a piece missing, it's still useable as long as both serial numbers are on each side. If one letter or number is missing from a tear ripped out, it is not accepted and is unusable.

If a bill is torn in half, repair it immediately by taping it. You don't want to lose one half. I always have scotch tape on hand for quick fix ups. If you're in a big rush or can't find tape, use the stapler and staple both halves together until you have time to tape them later.

In the office supply stores, I have seen specialty felt markers you can buy specifically for detecting fake paper money. Our bar used to carry the markers and the problems we encountered were that caps went missing and the pens dried out rather quickly. You can also buy money lights that when holding a bill under them, can detect fakes. They are inexpensive and can also be found in the office supply stores. I like to rely on myself and learn to detect the real from the fake money. It's also a handy skill to have since cash is transferred on a daily basis.

Did you know…?

The following are some random facts and fun information in relation to the bar industry.

Did you know…

1. When you pour a diet coke or coke from the gun, it foams up and it takes up too much time before the bubbles settle down until you can top the glass up. When you're busy, waiting for the bubbles to settle wastes precious time you may not have.

> *...grab a piece of lime and squeeze the juice overtop. It breaks down the bubbles very quickly and you can top up the soda and go!*

2. I take extra pints on my tray to sell when I get very busy. If they don't sell, it's given to the bartender to hold for me until a customer orders a pint. The longer the draft sits behind the bar, it settles, the head disappears and it looks flat.

> *...when a pint is ordered, I grab a straw and stir up the top portion of the beer to foam it up and give it some head. It looks freshly poured and the customer will never know. It's a good idea to ask your bartender to pour the pint of draft into a fresh, frosty pint glass.*

3. If you can't tell the difference between a drink which has soda/7-Up or water, look closely: the *pop has tiny bubbles in it, especially clinging to the straw.* If your eyesight is bad, do the straw test.

4. *Tonic water always glows and looks blue under the black light.*

5. *Diet coke looks slightly darker than regular coke.*

6. *Rye looks darker than white rum.*

7. When you make a paralyser (vodka, tequila, sambucca, or banana) drink, it could curdle if you don't follow these instructions:

Scoop ice into glass

Put shot of liquor in glass

Pour the coke in (about three-fourths full)

Wait until the coke settles and stops fizzing

Lightly pour the cream or milk in to fill up the rest of the glass.

…If you pour the cream in before the coke or pour the cream in while the coke is still fizzling, there's a good chance the drink will start to curdle.

8. If a customer asks you for a drink in a tall glass with no ice, watch your straw as you walk with your tray. There is *no ice to hold the straw in place* and by the time you arrive to the table, the straw will be laying on your tray or on the floor.

9. You should keep a box of baking soda on hand to neutralize and clean any stinky trays with a cork liner. Sprinkle a small amount on the surface and then add some hot water. Take an empty glass, flip it upside down and rub the soda into the tray. Rinse and wipe it dry. If you don't have baking soda, I find soda water works pretty good too. *Baking soda can be used on any tray to kill the stink.*

10. *Kitty litter is handy for soaking up puke on surfaces and it also neutralizes the smell.* Sprinkle it onto the area, let it soak and vacuum it up later.

11. *When soda pop is poured into a glass and it goes flat, there may be too much bleach in the dishwasher* where it coats the glassware while being washed. You'll know for sure when customers start to complain about a harsh bleach smell while taking a sip out of the glass.

12. When you open a *can of juice* such as pineapple or tomato, immediately pour it into a plastic container. If it's left in the can, within a couple of days it will start its *oxidization process* and go bad and it will also start smelling of tin.

13. *If you get a couple of drinks confused, use the "straw taste test."* This is when you take a straw, dip it into the drink, and cover the end with your finger. Keeping your finger over the straw, bring it to your mouth, remove your finger and the liquid will fall out.

If you still can't figure out which drink is which, ask your bartender. This is a great way to sample new drinks you've never tried.

14. A friend of mine who was in the military once told me a clean passport can be worth over $25,000.00 on the black market! *Try not to take your passport to the bar in case you lose it.*

15. Sometimes glassware can crack when you pour hot water or coffee into it. To keep this from happening, put a metal spoon into the glass and then pour the hot liquid in. *The spoon diffuses the heat and keeps the glass from breaking.*

16. Some establishments will not allow customers to be served while wearing a wife beater. My bartender went to Australia with his wife and he said that when they went into the bars there, there were signs which read, "No Singlets Allowed." He had to ask the bartender what it meant and was informed a singlet means a wife beater. For those of you who do not know what a *wife beater or singlet are, it's a man's tight ribbed tank top.*

17. *A bill with a hole ripped in the center was more than likely on a stripper's nipple.* A dancer receives a bill on stage as a tip and rips a hole into it so she can poke her nipple through it and parades around on stage with it. The guys love it and this gets the crowd throwing more money on stage for her.

18. *Ice in a drink makes it harder to spill.* If you're carrying a full tray of drinks and there is a martini, glass of wine, or drink with no ice, you may want to carry that drink in your free hand. You will have a better chance of it not spilling this way. If you're carrying out more than one drink with no ice, you'll have no choice but to carry it on your tray. You'll have to be steadier with the tray and walk smoothly so they don't spill.

19. *Lime cutters save large amounts of time and product.* It's a two-piece metal contraption that, when you place a full lime or lemon on the metal section and slam down the top part over the fruit, it sections it into eight evenly cut pieces. It's fast and keeps all pieces cut to the same size. In the past, staff would hand-cut limes and the pieces ended up either too large (to fit into a Corona bottle) or too small (consisting mostly of rind).

20. When placing dirty jugs onto the glass washer to be washed, you should *put the jug down with the handle facing the direction the glassware is traveling.* If you set them down the opposite way, the jugs fall down on their side and then they won't get the interior washed.

21. Contrary to what you've heard, *bars do not "water down" their alcohol.* When a shot is poured off the gun, it is calibrated, which means that when you press the button for a liquor, it pours out exactly an ounce. Sometimes the measure is off and it pours short of a shot. Other times it goes the opposite way and over-pours. It has to be manually set for the right amount to come out.

22. My new bartender gave me a really neat idea. He said when he worked at the nightclub, during a special celebration like a birthday party; he would take a short glass and pour some tonic water into it. Then he would light a tea-light and set it into the glass carefully until it floated. *With the black lights in the bar, the tonic water glowed in the dark with the little tea-light.* Setting a few of these out gives a nice little ambiance! He also mentioned if you add a shot of cranberry juice, it gives off a reddish glowing hue and a shot of lime cordial makes the liquid glow green. Neat effect to have around the Christmas season, I'm sure!

23. Sometimes draft beer can foam like crazy. It may have something to do with someone recently moving the keg

and stirring up the contents before it was hooked up. A short while ago, our bar was having that problem, so I decided to pick the brain of the guy who came out to fix the problem. He informed me sometimes the beer is not at the right temperature. It should be less than 40 degrees Fahrenheit, 38 degrees is perfect. The speed of the pour should be checked as well because too fast or too slow will cause it to foam.

24. Guys love to high-five each other and I have high-fived my share of people at the bar. I was recently told by a customer that the secret of never missing hands when you high-five someone is to watch the elbow of the person you're smacking hands with. He said, "Don't look at the hand, but do look at the elbow and you'll never miss. I learned this tip from a guy in a bar in Whistler," he commented to me. I now try it all the time and I've never missed yet!

25. When a customer takes the coaster from under their drink and sets it on top covering it, this is universal language for, "I'm coming back. Don't take my drink away. I'm not done with it yet."

Chapter 8
The Downside of Serving

The Bar Rules

Yuck, the dreaded bar rules. They are there for a few reasons which are to keep everyone safe, everyone on the same page and everything in check.

Rules exist for safety and privacy. Customers not touching the girls or using their cell phones at gyno are usually enforced. Most cell phones have a built in camera and video recorder and this makes it too easy for someone to post a picture of a dancer during her show onto the internet without her knowing. This rule is followed to respect her privacy since some dancers have children and sometimes their family members don't know what they do for a living. If a customer is found video taping or snapping a photo of a dancer, the DJ will usually go through the customer's phone and delete those videos and photos. On the other hand, since the dancer is doing a show and you're sitting at gyno, you should be paying attention to her and not texting away to a buddy.

Our establishment doesn't mind photos taken in the bar unless there's a dancer on stage at the same time. Female customers seem to be the only ones running around with cameras anyways and they can get quite defensive when asked to put their camera away. I like to explain to them that they're in a strip bar and there are many customers who want to be kept anonymous. They have wives and girlfriends who don't know they sneak in here from time to time and we want to respect their privacy. Most people are pretty understanding when you explain this to them. If they don't put the camera away, they're usually given a warning of being told to leave if it happens again.

Some bars don't allow bikers to bring their helmets into the bar because they can be used as a weapon in a fight (so I'm told). Helmets can usually be checked in with the bartender or left outside on the owner's bike depending on the bar. A bar which doesn't allow its customers to check in their helmets uses this as an excuse to deter the hardcore bikers from coming into the bar in the first place. Since these guys don't want to leave their helmets outside on their bikes to get stolen, they'll leave and find another bar to drink at. As bikers check in their helmets and jackets, they blend in better with the regular clientele and don't stand out as much, which may intimidate many women and some patrons. Some bikers may wear their club's patch on their jacket or vest which could start trouble with other members, so no "colors" is another rule many pubs and clubs keep. I know many of the local bikers and they know about and abide by our club's rules. They respect it and still visit, but without the label.

Every bar will have its own set of rules. Enforce them when you need to because if you let people get away with it one time, they will try to get away with it the next. It also upsets me when a customer says to me, "What's the big deal? The other waitress on nightshift lets me do it all the time!"

Don't be afraid of approaching customers about your bar rules. If you find someone with their feet on a table or chair, tell them to remove them immediately. This is your place of work, so be proud of it and respect it. If someone brings in their helmet and sets it down on an empty chair, ask him to please check it in with the bartender or remove it from the building. If wife beaters (a white ribbed undershirt in tank top style) are not allowed, ask the customer to kindly put on another shirt, put on a jacket or give him an extra beer shirt you have as promo.

Another standard rule is that every single customer who enters the bar must buy a drink. This doesn't mean it has to be alcoholic. It could be a bottle of water, a coffee, a soda or juice. Some people get upset with me when I tell them this. I explain that since we don't charge an entrance fee (cover charge), this is a rule enforced by management and is the way we pay the dancers.

The Carelessness of Drinking on Shift

Drinking on shift is illegal and can get you fired. A liquor inspector can come in at any time and do a walk through. Alcohol relaxes a person and causes motor skills and mental alertness to decrease. You'll have a hard time memorizing, it will make you feel tired and your ability to make proper work decisions such as monitoring your customer's level of drunkenness will diminish. So, if a customer is kind enough to buy you a cocktail or a beer, drink it after your shift (or better yet, just pocket the money).

The Stupidity of Stealing

I hate to write about this section since everyone already knows that stealing is wrong. I feel this is an important subject to touch upon as there are many different ways of stealing. If staff steals from customers, these customers will eventually stop coming into the bar and the bar ends up shutting down because it goes broke. If staff steals from the bar, the bar eventually goes broke and shuts down. If staff steals from other staff, good servers will eventually leave and go find work in another establishment. Remember to treat this as your business too!

Padding a tab is when a server charges a customer for drinks he didn't order or consume. People are not stupid and they know when they are being scammed. If you're in the habit of padding tabs, customers will complain to management and you will be watched, eventually caught and then fired. Karma has a way of catching up with you.

Calling out an order and not ringing in those drinks. The server pockets that money from the customer. This results in inventory being out and all staff being monitored and watched.

Another way of stealing is taking customers' or coworkers' personal belonging such as wallets, cell phones, jackets, etc. I know how thankful customers are when I pick up a cell phone left behind or a dropped wallet on the floor. The person gushes with gratitude. One of my regulars brought his brother in who was from out of town on a

Friday afternoon. My regular said, "This is Ro. She's my favourite waitress of all time! She's the one who found my wallet on the floor and gave it to me!" To this day, he leaves me very generous tips. Customers never forget.

Picking a tip up off a table that you didn't serve and keeping it for yourself is another way of stealing. If you start a shift after a server leaves or you take over another server's section and a tip is left on the table you didn't serve, be honest and give it to her or leave it in her box. She obviously worked hard for it and someone appreciated her service. She also has to tip everyone out.

The Dreaded Price Increase

There'll be times when the bar will increase its prices. This is inevitable and all servers must go through these times where customers complain and for a few weeks we seem to make less money. Before we know it, everyone gets used to the new price and customers adjust their tipping accordingly.

Sometimes prices go up by a few cents. Don't think that a few cents are not a big deal because it all adds up at the end of a shift. The sooner you let customers know about the increase in price, the sooner they get used to it. Many regulars have said to me, "Ro, every time you drop a beer off for me, make it $7.00." Now, what do I do when the price increases from $6.00 to $6.50? Do I still say something to the regular who is already giving me that dollar tip? Yes, I do. Dropping off the beer, I say, "Jim, just so you know the bar has increased their prices."

He'll ask, "Oh really, by how much?"

I would respond with, "Well, your Jack Daniels got raised by only fifty cents." I like to use the word *only*, so it doesn't seem like that big of a deal.

Some people find that fifty cents is a big deal and you'll have some customers make the annoying comment, "Well, I guess it comes out of your tip." One of my regulars got mad and made that same remark last price increase and I responded with, "Guess you start going to the bar for your beer from now on Larry." He looked at me in a stunned and funny way and decided to continue to tip me my usual amount. Of course I was only joking when I said that!

Don't be embarrassed to say something. The first week is hard, but before you know it, things eventually even out and end up working out. If customers moan, groan, and freak out on you, don't get mad or defensive. Don't start cursing the bar and jump on their bandwagon. Calmly explain that unfortunately the bar has to keep up with other local business' prices and inflation always has a way to catch up. Be business-like and professional about it.

It Sucks to Get Stiffed

We're in this business to make money and while working in this industry, servers put up with a lot so you need to grow a thick skin and quick. Most of the time, you'll make a tip and then there are the times where you won't. That's the way it is.

It's maddening when you run your butt off for someone; you're friendly and seem to have a great rapport with them, only for them to leave you nothing on the tip line or the table. That's the chance you take. Tip doesn't stand for '*you have to tip me now.*' But, customers do have to understand we're there to make money.

Customers want to constantly buy us drinks. That's great and all but 99 percent of us prefer cold hard cash. That really rocks our boat. It's really frustrating for me as a server when a guy is buying himself and his buddy beer after beer, putting a couple quarters on my tray (worse yet, nothing at all) and all the while placing big bills on stage for every dancer who walks up there… and this is ongoing for a couple of hours. At times like that I wish I was allowed to say, "Thanks a lot. If you can afford to tip every dancer $20.00, why can't you tip me a little more than a measly fifty cents? You ask ME to give you change for your twenties so you can give them to the dancers, sometimes robbing me of all my fives. You ask me to put your order of food into the kitchen or bring you nonstop glasses of water. I drag out your nice cold beer, being courteous to put a coaster down for you while I clean up your empties and carry them back to the bar. I also bring you cutlery, napkins, ketchup, salt and pepper and I make an extra trip back to the kitchen to get you that extra dip you want. Your dirty dishes and all the condiments must be taken away again. Sometimes you spill something by accident and I am there to clean up the mess for you. I'm sure you don't know that I have to tip out the DJ, the bartender, the kitchen, the house and a doorman if he's on shift with that *generous* fifty cent tip."

Serving It Right and Other Mandatory Self-study Courses

Before you're allowed to work as a server in British Columbia, you're required by law to take Serving It Right (servingitright.com). It's a wonderful self-study package which informs a person of British Columbia's responsible serving program. Once you've read the materials and do the exam online, by mail, fax or in person, you must pass to receive a plastic certification card. A person holding this card is legally allowed to work in an establishment serving liquor. The course is extremely helpful and will shed some insight on the importance of being responsible in serving alcoholic beverages to the public, the consumption of alcohol and the legalities involved.

It's a good idea to get your certificate before you apply for a job. This way, you could be hired instead of someone else who might have been chosen (who doesn't hold the certificate yet) but they chose you because you could start immediately. If you're outside the province of British Columbia, you'll want to find out about your provincial serving laws or the laws in your state or country.

Asking Customers for Identification

The following is some helpful information regarding decisions a server must make in relation to the identification process and safety of her patron. This is from a British Columbia standpoint. You'll want to check with your manager or head waitress to find out about any identification that is acceptable or unacceptable at your bar.

To aid you in checking identification you have not seen before (out of province) and you're not sure if it's valid or not, your bar can get hold of a manual that shows examples and explains in detail what other province's driver's licenses look like in Canada. We also have a second manual that shows driver's licenses from the United States. Keep the manual handy so you're able to compare out-of- province driver's licenses to see if they're fake or real.

Our bar wants us to check identification on anyone who looks thirty years old and younger. I have asked people for their identification only to find out they're older than I am! Other times I'm looking at someone thinking, "They've got to be way over the legal age," only to second-guess myself and decide to check anyways. Many times I'm amazed to find out they had just turned nineteen and already look like they're much older than I originally thought. Never be ashamed or embarrassed to ask someone for their identification. Your job is on the line.

Before the start of a shift, know the exact date. Once in a while I have this feeling that something looks *"off"* about an ID while I'm inspecting it. As I let it sink into my brain, I realize the person is underage and they're hoping you don't know how to count. When I call them on it, some say, "Oh, I thought the legal age is 18. I'm from Alberta."

My reply is, "Then why are you carrying a B.C. driver's license?"

In a group of young people, if one or more of them look underage don't single that one person or people out. I ask every single person in the group to pull out two pieces of ID. The reason for this is that the younger-looking patrons in the group could *"borrow"* that older buddy's identification if they forgot theirs or they really are underage.

When I start to inspect everyone's ID, I'm actually reading the first and last name to myself as I'm reading the rest of the ID. This way, if John Doe gave me a driver's license and a care card and then the fifth guy in the group also named John Doe gave me a passport and a credit card, I will have made the connection. I know one guy in the group gave his buddy some of his other pieces of ID. This way I ask everyone to kindly pull out their identification for me a second time. Don't be embarrassed to make them all go through this process again. If you hear groaning and protesting, they know they've got a smart server they can't fool! It's a good feeling and it's impressive, even to the youngsters. When young people can constantly fool a bar, the word will spread to their friends and more of them will attempt it as a result. When that happens, it takes months to get it under control where the kids stop trying.

There are many forms of identification and you want to be able to distinguish the fakes from the real thing.

Looking for the Fakes

Looking at a driver's license, you want to keep an eye out for anything that looks peculiar. Years ago, kids had been altering their driver's licenses and their B.C identification cards' last digit by scraping it from the number eight to a six. If you take the license and check it from all angles by letting light shine onto it, you'll be able to see scratch marks. I've asked kids how they would explain this to a cop if he were to notice this. Nobody had an answer for me, just a shrug of the shoulders.

Take a second look at anything you don't recognize. I have seen ID signed with BLUE pen! I look at the youngster and say, "Honey, I'm sorry. You really got ripped off on this ID. Where did you get it?" He knows he's been busted.

"Downtown" he says as he looks at me sheepishly.

"How much did you pay for it?" "$50.00"

"Come back when you're 19." You really do have to laugh and can't blame them for trying!

If you really are unsure about a piece of ID, take it to the bar and ask the bartender or another server to have a peek at it and give you a second opinion.

A Canadian Citizenship card needs to be taken under the black light where you will notice a glowing hologram of the maple leaf.

Years ago, three young guys from Guatemala came into the bar and they handed me Guatemalan ID. One of our doormen was originally from Guatemala and while he was having lunch in the bar on his day off, I was able to ask him to have a look at the ID.

What they had given me wasn't considered a piece of government ID. My doorman was able to communicate to them that they were not allowed to stay with that form of ID unless they showed us a passport. They left.

Always get a second or third opinion. If you're unsure, it's better to tell the person to leave than serve him and the liquor inspector or cops end up coming in.

During slow times, pull out any identification you have in your wallet and take it into the dark of the bar and then into the black light. Play around with it and inspect it further under different lighting so you have an inkling of what a real ID looks like. Some bars keep all altered ID that were confiscated in a box or drawer somewhere and you can take this out and inspect it as well to get a better understanding of what the fakes look like. If you don't have a Canadian citizenship card, ask regulars in the bar if you can take a peek at theirs and tell them what you're doing. You just want to get familiar with all sorts of ID.

When asking someone for identification, their main piece should be Government issued with their picture and signature on it. It should not be expired. A passport is fine, but if the person looks like they're five years old in the photo, it's not acceptable since it's expired. Same goes for a Canadian Citizenship card, which I myself have and I'm eight years old with braids in the photo! I've obviously never had it updated and it still has my maiden name on it.

A **primary** piece of identification must contain the customer's name, signature and a picture.

Acceptable- Driver's license, passport, B.C. identification, Firearms Weapons card, Indian Status card, Military identification, Canadian Citizenship card.

I will accept a credit card with a photo on it, but it must be backed up with at least two other pieces of identification.

Not Acceptable- Gym membership identification, Costco card, school identification, etc.

A **second** piece of ID must include the customer's name and a signature on the back.

Acceptable- A bank card, credit card, Care card, S.I.N. card.

N*ot Acceptable-* A blank bank card with no name imprinted on the front, Library card, Air Miles card, Gas points card, etc.

If you're unsure, ask another staff member. It's better to be safe than sorry. I will not accept any photocopied identification as it could have been altered in some way, and then photocopied, and you wouldn't be able to tell. If you're young and expecting to be asked for ID, you should have it on you at all times anyways and definitely not have anything photocopied.

Every single person needs to carry some forms of ID on them. If that person got in trouble or an accident, the cops may need to get a hold of a wife or parent. Even if you look like you're eighty years old and you don't have one piece of ID on yourself, don't be surprised if you won't be allowed into a pub or bar.

What to look for:

Photo

When someone hands you their primary piece of ID, you want to make sure you take a good look at the person and then at the picture. Don't worry about hair color as people color their hair and change their style all the time. Look at the overall face shape and compare the nose. If you have any doubts, ask for a few more pieces of ID or ask a coworker for a second opinion. If I have any doubts the ID belongs to the customer, he is told to leave.

Birth date

Make sure you know today's date. Anyone who turns legal age tomorrow is still underage as of today. Don't give the poor guy a hard time as he's probably trying to get in on a Saturday night and hang out with his buddies and his birthday is the next day being Sunday.

Expiry Date

Almost any ID that has an expiration date should be honored. If it is expired, it is considered invalid.

Secondary piece of ID

The piece should have the customer's name and a signature that you can compare to the photo ID. A care card is a great second piece of identification since it contains the person's name and birth date, as well as their signature.

***ALWAYS remember… if you have any doubts about a person's identification, you have the right to refuse entry.

Dealing With Problem Customers

The problem customer is the person who must leave the premises before they're given a drink. Not only are these people a pain in the neck to deal with, they could also be a liability to the business. Problem people include:

Barred Patron

This is the person who has caused problems in the past such as fighting, vandalism (vandalizing vehicles or the restrooms, for example), harassing, or threatening staff and other customers. When a person is barred, it means they're not allowed back into the bar, sometimes on a probationary period, other times forever.

Intoxicated Patron

Sometimes a drunk who has been drinking in another establishment and has been cut off, may come straight to your bar if he wants to continue his drinking binge instead of going home. That person needs to leave your premises immediately or you're responsible for them once they're served a drink. Call a cab for this person and get him home.

Customers Ordering Many Drinks in One Sitting

When a customer sits down and orders a jug of beer, I need to ask him how many glasses are needed. Sometimes friends are joining him so he may respond with two or more. Then there are times where he will say, "Just one for me."

It is illegal to serve one jug to one customer because it is a large amount of alcohol for one person at one time. Some people have a hard time monitoring their drinking at a moderate pace.

Ask your manager or senior server about serving triples in your bar. I tell customers we don't allow it. There really is no reason why a person needs to drink triples other than to get completely loaded. You don't need the loaded customer sitting in your bar, puking on the stage and passing out. I'm aware and get antsy when a person orders double cocktails in short glasses with lots of ice while drinking three or more in the matter of less than an hour. Keep conversing with your bartender, shooter girl and any other servers to monitor any customer's vast amounts of alcohol intake.

Cutting Patrons Off

One of the reasons people go to the bar is to celebrate a birthday, engagement, divorce, etc by drinking. Some people can't seem to hold their alcohol and they drink too quickly in a short amount of time. A celebration like a birthday or stag party has one person as the center of attention and things can get out of hand rather quickly if you're not keeping a close eye on the group. Most stag parties are great to serve but sometimes there's the party who simply starts to get out of hand, where guys are buying rounds of shots and drinks for the whole group and it's almost like a game of everyone wanting their turn to buy a round for everyone else. Before you know it, there is empty shooter glasses scattered all over the place and everyone has three full drinks in front of them. The thrifty guys usually send drinks only to the groom or birthday boy and it is this person who ends up looking at a handful of full beers and shooters staring at him.

I know that I've already mentioned the signs of a customer who has had too much to drink under "The Drunk", but I want to touch on them once more since this is a very important subject. You as a server needs to be fully aware of all your customers. A person who needs to be cut off (stop serving him immediately) has many noticeable signs. The indications that point at the customer who's in a drunken state are slurred, mumbled, or loud speech, or even opposite: fast talking. Coordination isn't present, such as trouble picking up change off the table. Eyes may be half closed, glassy, bloodshot, blank stare which is staring at nothing in particular, nodding off as if falling asleep, and may jerk his head back up. His complexion may be beet red in color and as he sits in his chair, he may sway side to side and not sit still. Throwing up at the table is a big sign since he is usually too drunk to make it to the restroom. As drunk people walk, they may weave, stumble or shuffle and even walk into a chair, table or another person. As they walk with a drink in their hand, sometimes it seems to spill all over their hand because they can't seem to keep their hand steady.

Some important tips when cutting someone off

- In a group where one person seems to be very intoxicated, I let the group know hey won't be served anymore until the intoxicated person leaves the building. The reason for this is because guys in the group will continue sneaking the drunk more alcohol even when you tell him their friend is cut off. A few times I've let people continue to buy drinks for themselves, at the same time I threaten to kick them all out if I find out anyone is sneaking beers to the drunk. Most of them try to be sneaky and continue buying drinks for the drunk anyways. They think it's funny or they can't seem to reason with their drunken friend who is demanding more alcohol. Some guys want to get their friend so inebriated so he can't stand anymore, so my trying to be the nice guy ends up biting me in the ass.

It's just easier to cut the whole group off in the first place until the drunk is taken home.

• Years ago, I had a bartender who would continue serving the guys who I cut off if they went to his bar. His reasoning was that the guy didn't seem that drunk to him. I was always the one who said, "I told you so!!" when we end up kicking him out. When another staff member serves a patron who has been cut off, it makes the staff member who cut him off in the first place look like they don't know how to do their job. Even if that server ends up being wrong in their decision, you honour that and stand behind them.

• When you cut someone off, you must let all other staff know immediately. You want to tell all fellow servers (in case this person moves to their side of the room), the shooter girl, bartenders, the DJ and even doormen. This way, everyone is aware of this person, should he happen to leave the premises and drive away in their own vehicle, fight, fall asleep, etc.

• Always offer this person a free coffee, water, or pop. I like to engage in conversation by asking what their mode of transportation is to get home. Sometimes there's a friend in the room who is looking after them, but there are times when the person is drinking solo. Offer to call a taxi or ask if they need to use the phone to call someone to pick them up. We have a program where someone comes to pick up the customer and his car and get their car home for them safely. It's your legal responsibility as server to make sure this person has a safe way home.

• If I notice an intoxicated person walk into the bar and sit down, I greet him and if I even have an inkling of him being intoxicated, I'll ask if they have been drinking. Usually they will say that they've had a couple. At that point I respond with, "I'm sorry; you've had too much to drink today. I can't serve you. Sorry but you'll have to leave," and walk away. Don't stand there as they'll start to argue with you. Walk over to the bartender immediately and tell him what happened. He will honour your decision if the customer ends up going to the bar and tries ordering a drink from him. The bartender will be ready to tell the person to go.

• Never take a bribe for allowing someone or his friend to stay and drink if the patron is underage or has no ID. I've been offered as much as $300.00 to let a group's buddy stay while the friend has no ID to prove he is of age.

• Never allow someone to intimidate you into letting them stay.

Example: "Do you have any idea who I am/know?!"

"Where's Cindy? I know her. She always lets me stay!"

• Be polite when talking to someone and telling them you suspect them of having too much to drink that day. I've had a friend of the person pull me aside and tell me his friend is mentally handicapped. It's rare if I'm wrong, but I'm just looking out for the bar's liquor license.

Problems with Coworkers

Things don't always run smoothly between staff members during a shift. When problems arise, any disputes must be ironed out and dealt with quickly so you can both get on with your jobs. Never get into a screaming match out in the bar where customers can witness it since it looks extremely unprofessional. If you must, take it to the staff room and sort it out.

During a shift, each server will be responsible for her section of the room containing tables. Look at these tables as income for that server on that particular shift. Servers are very territorial over their sections so the sooner a new server realizes this, there will be fewer troubles. During slow periods of a shift, if a customer were to stop me and order a drink from another server's section, I'll let that server know about the drink order so she can take it out and receive the tip. If the room is bubbling with energy and all servers are busy, take the drinks out so the customers aren't kept waiting. Usually the other server won't mind if you tell her you took a drink out to her section because she was on the other side of the room or looked like she was carrying out a full tray of drinks at the time. Don't be sneaky about it; be vocal and explain yourself.

Years ago we used to have a server who was always late starting her shift. She assumed the time started was the time she could sit on the toilet, make a phone call or apply her lipstick. I didn't mind in the beginning because I was making tips, but after a while I got sick of it since she was taking advantage of me. I told her from then on I will expect her to be on time for her shift so I can go on my break or go home when I'm supposed to, not a minute later. If I kept my mouth shut, it would've gone on forever, not to mention she was signing in to get paid her wage the time I was still working the floor. She was another girl who didn't last long with us.

Years later, an argument broke out between me and another server. She was another girl whom I remember getting mad at for showing up late for a shift too many times in a row to relieve me from my shift. One day she came in and I greeted her with a hello. She ignored me and I couldn't help myself and say, "Are you still mad at me for freaking out on you a couple of days ago for being constantly late?"

She looked at me and said, "Ya Romana, I am. You didn't have to yell at me."

I responded with, "Well, get used to it. You pull that again and I may be yelling at you again!" I admit that I shouldn't have lost my temper and yelled again, but I didn't think she would take it too personally.

We all have to work together and I used to joke to the regulars and staff I see more of them than I do of my own husband. All I can say is "Get over it!" It makes working with the person you got into a fight with very uncomfortable, so stop the unnecessary drama of holding a grudge. Get on with life and get back to work.

Customers who run tabs may have a few different servers add drinks to their tab in the course of a visit. A server may end up going off shift or on a break, so another server will take over and there may be a shooter girl adding shots. If the customer ends up leaving a tip, it should be split up accordingly to the drinks each server has on the tab. One of my pet peeves is when I sell a tab to another server and I don't find tip money in my box (when I know the customers are regulars and always leave a tip). I hate asking that server, "Remember the tab I had with the guys drinking double Grey Goose sodas at gyno? Did they leave a tip?"

It's even more annoying when the response is, "Ya, I owe you a fifteen dollar tip."

Don't ever make a server ask you for her money!! It is rude, embarrassing and annoying. Even if the tip is a quarter, drop it into her box with a note saying the quarter is from table #29 or whomever. I like to staple any paper money to the bill or scrap paper and I put her name on it. This shows her who left her a tip and how much. Don't ever leave loose bills in a server's box because sometimes other servers may end up using her box if she's not working and any loose money will be collected by the wrong server. This way, if there is a paper or bill stapled to cash, the new server borrowing the box knows it doesn't belong to her and she'll return it.

I know my regulars and it makes me a little suspicious when girls say that certain regulars didn't leave a tip that night, when for the last twelve years (or whatever length of time I I've known them), they've always been more than generous. Don't insult another waitress like this by lying and ripping her off. She'll eventually find out the truth. Liars and cheaters don't last long in this business.

Other Problems with Customers

The interesting part of this job is dealing with many different personalities while extraordinary incidents happen in the course of a shift.

You work in a bar; people hit on you. Get used to it! Instead of being mad about it, be flattered people find you attractive. Yes, I said 'people'. I've been hit on by not only men, but women as well. I've been told on a couple of occasions that they find my raspy voice very sexy. It does get a little weird when a woman rubs your arm and tells you how soft your skin is while she leans into you or even grabs your bum! Yup, that's happened to me as well.

Working as a server in a strip bar, you will always get asked by guys "When are you up?" On occasion, coworkers still ask me, "Ro, do you still get asked when you're getting up on stage?"

"Of course I still do," I reply.

"Doesn't it make you mad?" they ask again.

"No. I've been asked that question a thousand times. I guess I'm just used to it by now. I actually find it flattering."

At times you'll be asked by customers where they can buy weed or coke. Everyone assumes that since you work in this wild and crazy industry, you have all the connections and you're involved in this stuff yourself. I know stuff and I don't know stuff. I don't get involved and I don't care what people are up to as it's none of my business. I don't know if the person asking me is an undercover cop or a guy passing through town. I just tell people, "I'm sorry, I can't help you." The persistent person pushes with, "Oh come on, you know. Just tell me! There's a big tip in it for you!" Like I said before, "I don't get involved, so I don't know." I can only advise you to follow the same rule. If your manager or the owner were to find out you're getting involved in this kind of thing in their business, you'll end up being fired.

Handling a customer with bad body odour is a real tricky topic to have to deal with. You need to do it in a professional manner and in a way where it doesn't embarrass the customer because you want them to return. Most of these people obviously don't notice their own offensive odour or they just don't care they offend others around them. This problem came up at my work a few years ago. The best way to deal with this person is to ask your manager to go over and let that person know people have complained about his foul smelling body odour. This man apologized like crazy and said he was on his way home from work when he decided to pop by our bar for a quick beer. He downed his beer and left immediately. I got onto this subject with my husband and we agreed this was the best way to handle the situation because if it came from a female server, he might have taken it more personally.

Working in this industry, you will come in contact with the intoxicated Drunks. These are the people who stumble around the bar almost knocking into your tray as they meander around the room in search of a buddy or convince a waitress to serve them one last drink. Some will start to fall asleep in their chair or attempt a fight with other patrons. This is the person you will have to babysit until a taxi, ride, or friend arrives to pick him up.

Many times you'll be dealing with a birthday party or a stag. The mission of the guy's friends is to get the groom or birthday boy absolutely gooned so the poor guy can't remember his own name. This is when you need to keep an eye out for the puker. I do my best to remind the groom or birthday boy throughout his visit to let me know if he needs a water, coffee or pop. Before the floodgates open I like to warn the friends, "I do not want him puking on the carpets. I'm warning you guys that I do not clean up puke. If he throws up, someone in this group WILL be cleaning up after him!" I never have a problem when I warn them.

It's impossible to satisfy every single person who sets foot in your bar. I could be working a busy Saturday night and the partiers are loud and having a great time. Then two old guys will enter and complain at how loud the music is and they can't hear each other talk. People have complained the air conditioning is too cold while others complain the room is too hot at the same time. I've had customers grumble the beef dip wasn't very good, yet everything was polished off the plate but the plate itself. This is the complainer. Keep in mind, you'll always get someone who is unhappy, enjoys complaining or is out to try and get a free meal or drink.

Here is another customer who you will eventually meet; the one lonely guy whose girlfriend just broke up with him and he just lost his job, so he's drinking his sorrows away. Then he thinks its okay to meander around the room and join people at their tables trying to make new friends. Instead of making friends, he's slurring at everyone and interrupting circles of people trying to talk and have a relaxing time. I'll usually lean over to someone in the group and ask if he's bothering them. If I get an indication (or someone comes up to me and asks me to tell him to leave them alone), then I'll pull the socialiser aside and tell him he can't be interrupting others since I'm getting complaints. Sometimes he gets the hint while other times he doesn't. If he continues to disrupt others at their tables, you need to form a plan and get him out of the bar before a fight erupts. I'll usually tell the socialiser I'm going to call him a taxi and it's time for him to go home.

What to Do if a Customer Won't Leave When You Ask Him To

Yes, there will be times when you'll have problems with the young, just as you'll have problems with everyone else.

An upset customer who is told he's not allowed to stay will demand to see the manager so he can explain why he has no ID on himself. He'll try convincing the manager to let him stay. Most times, the manager isn't in until the night shift anyways. Depending on how busy I am, I sympathize with him and tell him it's nothing personal since I'm just doing my job. I also point to the sign on the wall and mention the laws regarding identification have gotten stricter. Some staff members have even told people that if they go home and come back later with their ID, we'll buy them their first beer.

Sometimes you'll end up with a patron whom you can't reason with as he continues to explain a fourth time why it's not his fault he doesn't have his ID. At this point, I'm very annoyed because I don't like the drama and the scene he's making and he's wasting my time when I could be serving my customers and making money. This is when I've spent too much of my valuable time arguing and respond by saying, "Okay, time to go!"

If he keeps arguing, I respond with, "Buddy, I've got a lot of power in this room. I can cut you off, kick you out or even bar you! I'm the person whom you should be making friends with, not making mad!" If he refuses to calm down at this point, I'll say, "You know what? I have an excellent memory for remembering faces! Next time I won't even allow you to set foot in this bar even if you do have your ID with you!"

This usually shuts his trap because his friends are yelling at him to be quiet and apologizing to me for their friend's rude behaviour as they push him out the door. Most people don't behave this badly but I have had many episodes exactly like this one.

You don't want to be a bitch about it, but don't let people walk all over you or intimidate you. You need to stay in control and hold the upper hand. After all, you're there to do your job.

Another way the underage kids or kids with no ID try to fly under the radar is have a friend go buy drinks at the bar while they sit down. They're hoping you won't be fast enough to come and ask them for ID. Once their friend arrives at their table with the jug, he thinks that by pouring himself a glass and starting to drink, he's now allowed to stay.

"Buddy, you got your ID on you?" I'll ask.

"We already bought the jug." he'll respond.

I'll try again. "Do you have your ID? If you don't, you can't stay."

"This is bull! We already paid for the jug. We'll finish drinking it and then we'll go."

"No you won't. If you don't leave, I'll take the jug away and your friend won't even get to finish it. Then I'll call someone over to physically remove you." I'll respond as I smile. The person with no ID will leave and sometimes the guy who paid for the jug will stay and finish drinking it.

Dumb Things People Say and How to Deal With It

Ok, the more I thought about this section, the more I thought this particular topic needed its own chapter. Some of these scenarios have happened to me on more than a dozen occasions. When I mention them to other servers, they anxiously nod their heads and laugh at me saying, "Oh my God! That has happened to me too!"

You Have the Pull and Power in the Room

Some customers are rude and don't understand that just because you serve drinks, you should be looked upon as their slave or talked down to. I've had people yell at me to "f-off" when I cut them off or demand I get them a drink without using their manners. If a customer is demanding and rude, they're obviously forgetting I have pull and power in the bar. Do you think I'm going to give them a coffee or a bottle of water for free when they need it? How about a pop or a free shooter for their buddy's birthday? I'm asked to convince dancers to give posters to people because it's their birthday. If you're nice to me, I'll do everything I can to help you out. If you're not, don't hold your breath. Even for lunch draws, I'll make sure the loser doesn't end up with a winning ticket! Yes, I throw the other half into the trash.

As server, you'll have to go with the flow and try not to miss a beat. Yes, it's annoying when you walk up to a new customer and say, "Hi guys! What can I grab for you?" and they respond with "What? You're grabbing me where?" or "What? Where can I grab you?" especially when you're crazy busy and don't have time to play this game. Just smile and move on.

Unpredictable Scenarios You May Find Yourself In

I took some of the scenarios I've explained and made them into multiple choice questions where you guess the right answer. Hope you enjoy it!

"You should change your price so I can tip you better!"

This comment can drive a server to the edge of a cliff when she hears it! The drink is $4.95 and after the customer hands you a ten, you give him a nickel and five loonies. What do you respond with after he makes this idiotic comment?

a) "I don't make the prices, management does."
b) The only thing you can do is laugh in his face and walk away.
c) "Are you dense? Why the hell did I just break up the five dollar bill in coin, dummy?"

The right answer is a. You should still be polite and realize he obviously didn't want to tip you anyways. There may still be a small chance he'll tip you next time or perhaps leave some change on the table when he leaves.

"Why aren't you smiling?"

I've mentioned this one on more than one occasion throughout this book.

a) "Because I'm working and I hate it here!"
b) Smile and say, "I'm just busy concentrating."
c) "Give me something to smile about!"

The right answer is b. In the end, you're hoping for a tip so be polite. If you don't want anyone even making this comment in the first place, put a smile on.

"Can we ask you a personal question?"

I know it won't be anything like, "Have you ever been to Hawaii?" or "Do you like sushi?"

a) "No!" and storm away.
b) "Okay, let me have it!"
c) Try to keep a little humour in it and say, "If you're going to ask me if my boobs are real, they are. No, this is not my natural hair color. Yes, I'm married, and No, I will not tell you my age." Smile and walk away without waiting for

a response. You'll be smiling because they'll just sit there gaping at you.

The right answer is c. In my experiences, those are the four main questions I'm usually asked so that is my response. I don't say it in a mean way, just a matter of fact kind of tone. I don't want them upset with me where I screwed myself out of a tip. (You can even try b, if you're curious).

"When are you up on stage next?" or "Do you dance?"

This question doesn't bother me in the least. It's the following question that drives me nuts:

"Why not?"

a) "Because who's going to serve you drinks if I'm up on stage dancing? I don't want you guys to die of thirst."
b) "Because I don't want to show strangers my hooch."
c) "Because my husband wouldn't like it very much."

If you're still working for a tip, I suggest to be nice and your answer should be a.

"Does your husband tell you you're beautiful every day?"

I love this one because I can honestly answer, "As a matter of fact, he does!" I'll go along with my little game…

a) "As a matter of fact, he does!"
b) "No. What an asshole! Maybe I should dump him!"
c) "Actually, he slaps me around every night and kicks me in the stomach."

Just answer the guy with a, whether it's true or not.

"If you were my wife, I'd never let you work here."

a) "Well, it's a good thing we're not married then, huh?!"
b) "Actually, my husband hates that I work here too."
c) Start to cry and walk away.

First off, I think this is a very rude thing to say to someone. My response to this person is a. Straight and simple. My pride is worth more than his stinking tip. Besides, it's nobody else's business but mine.

"I haven't been asked for ID in years! I feel so young!"

I feel like kicking people in the shin when they say this to me because these are the people who look like they're 12 years old and have been frequenting the bar for only a couple of years.

a) I just hold my hand out for them to pass me their ID. Keep smiling!
b) "Ok buddy … you look like you're nine years old. So, just pass over the ID!"
c) "So, who hasn't been doing their job and not asking you for your ID?"

The right answer is a. Don't be rude if you want to end up with a tip.

"Does the girl on stage have real or fake boobs?"

First of all, I'm busy serving drinks and not paying attention to the girl that's parading around on the stage.

a) "Let me feel them and I'll let you know."
b) "I'll ask the dancer and get back to you about that!"
c) "Sorry, no idea."

A tip is what you're aiming for so the right answer is c.

"I'd buy you a bigger wedding ring"

This is another statement I find rude and irks me to the core! He is dumbfounded as I respond with, "I love my ring! My husband insisted I pick out what I liked. Besides, I don't like big, gaudy-looking rings." But, for the sake of this fun quiz, I'll continue…

a) "You would?! Boy, I'm missing out then."
b) "Buddy, you're not impressing me. Why don't you hit the highway?!"
c) "I love my ring! My husband insisted I pick out what I like."

My answer is c. Out of all the guys who have asked to see my ring, I've had two guys reply with, "What an exquisite cut!"

"Can I take you out for dinner sometime?"

I know it takes some guys a lot of guts to ask a girl out, so I will answer him with, "Thank you. I'm really very flattered but I'm married."

I've had a few guys respond with, "Well, then how about if we go out for coffee?"

At this point, I need to explain to him that my husband wouldn't be happy with me going out for dinner or coffee with strange men.

"Well, it's not like anything is going to happen," will be the response.

This is when I tell this person that I really don't have any time and any time that I do have available, I'd like to spend it with friends who I don't see enough of anyways.

"Boy! You must just love getting paid to work and watch this at the same time!"

We used to have duos on stage once a week every Thursday night. This was many years ago and the duo nights have long been cancelled since they are now illegal and the agency can't seem to find girls who want to do it anymore, anyways. Back then, most of the girls were pretty nasty and basically did a live sex show on the stage.

I've had a few guys make this stupid comment to me when I ask them at gyno whether they want another drink. Guys have said to me, "Boy! You must just love getting paid to work and get to watch this at the same time!" They're serious. I guess they thought I had a penis under my mini skirt!

"Do I get free water or pop because I'm a designated driver?"

If the guy is a limo or bus driver for a big group of people, he gets all the free pop, coffee, or water he wants. In my experience, these drivers never abuse this courtesy and usually have only one non- alcoholic drink (probably because they don't want to be worrying about running to a restroom for the rest of the evening).

Usually, the person who makes this comment came in with one friend and I respond with a "No, sorry."

If he starts to argue with me and tells me it's against the law, I shut him down and say, "Almost everyone in this bar is driving home tonight at some time. The bar's policy is that every single person must buy one drink to be in here. It's the way we pay the dancers."

If he still continues to argue, I continue with, "I don't make the rules. And since we don't charge cover, everyone must buy one drink. It can also be a coffee, pop or a bottle of water." I've made my point.

"Fine, I'll just get a Budweiser then." This is when I feel like kicking him in the leg.

"I thought you were driving?!" I'll say before I walk away. In my experience, this is the person who won't tip since he was too cheap to purchase a drink in the first place.

Action Steps to a Dine and Dash

Every waitress at one time or another will encounter a dine and dash. This is when a customer will consume something he's ordered or he'll run a tab without you grabbing a credit card and then he leaves you with the bill.

First off, your heart will drop or the blood will feel like it's draining from your face. Try not to panic. These are the action steps I take to see if I can save the situation and still get my money.

1. I leave my tray at the bar and tell the bartender I may have had a dine and dash. This way he will keep an eye on any drinks and my coin on the tray. Also, if I'm working with any other servers, they will understand why my tray may be in their way.

2. I run to the patron's table to look for signs that they may be returning. Look for a jacket, keys or cell phone. If there are no personal belongings and the drink is empty, it's time to form a quick strategy.

3. I stop and glance around the room for him. He may have moved to another table to sit with friends or a chair closer to the stage. If I don't see him, I run near the bar in case he went to the restroom and then returned to pay his bill. If the bartender isn't waving me over or waving money in the air, I know the customer has not gone to the bar.

4. Next, I run straight outside to see if he is in the smoking area or getting into his vehicle. I will even walk into the parking lot to have a better look.

5. If I'm satisfied he's not outside, I run back inside and ask a male to go into the washroom to see if there is anyone inside and then ask the description of the person inside.
6. If I still can't find him, I go back into the bar a second time and look at the customers in the room again. This is just in case he returned from the restroom.
7. By this point I am sure the person has left. On the bill I write my name and the date. On the back of the bill I write a description of the customer in detail. Then I give myself a moment and visualize him in case he does come back so I know who it is. I let all servers and bartender know what happened.
8. Some people come back later or the next day and realize they left on their bill. When this happens, I take the cash the customer gives me and the bill and staple both together. Then I drop it into the server's waitress box. What a nice surprise for her when she comes in for her next shift!

To avoid the scenario above, always grab a credit card and driver's license to run any tabs. This way, if the customer leaves by accident, it will be less likely he will cancel his driver's license and the credit card. Also, you will have proof he was physically in your bar and the cards were not stolen.

Romana Van Lissum

Bonus
Why Men Like To
Hang Out in Strip Bars

During the course of writing this book, I started to research some reasons as to why people like to hang out in strip bars as often as they do. I knew some of the reasons already because regulars would tell me over the years why they keep coming back. The main reason being the staff (the friendliness and the customers feel like they know them), and the familiarity of the bar (it feels like a second home to them). The quality of dancers is another reason and so is the food.

The "Why's" of Men

During my employment at the strip bar, I would pick my husband's brain on the 'WHY'S' of men. The answer is simple. It always comes down to sex and naked women. We all know men are visual creatures, there is no other secret.

Recently, I had a chat with some of my regulars who asked me if I would put a chapter into this book explaining this industry and some of the misconceptions many people have about the strippers and this industry. It got my brain thinking so I decided to do some research on the subject.

I know this book is for the waitress and how to make money, but I wanted to put some light on this subject since this job has been very good to me and got me financially to where I'm at. I don't like to hear people trash on this industry I have worked so long in, so I am here as a spokesperson. I see what is going on while serving drinks, watching what is happening around me.

Most of the readers who will pick up this book will be women and many will have boyfriends or husbands. The information I know about will shed some light and put some perspective onto this mysterious industry many know little about.

The majority of the public seem to think all strip bars are sleazy and seedy. They think the strippers are all on drugs and want to screw every guy who walks in the room. They probably have an inch more respect for the waitress, but not much.

I'm not a cop or a lawyer and it's not my business as to where the money comes from, so I have no problems with taking money from any of my customers; the clean money and the dirty money. I don't care whether a lawyer or mechanic gives me a tip or a drug dealer or biker does. If you feel like you can't sleep at night taking a tip from the bad boys, maybe you should change your line of work. All money has the EXACT same value and it pays the bills!

The Bars Give Back to the Community

Every year around the holidays, some of the local strip bars give back to the community and run fundraisers to raise money for their local food hampers. It's amazing to read some of the letters sent to the local papers from some little old bitty who says all the money we raise is dirty and should not be accepted.

A few Christmases ago, we were advertising for our annual fund raiser and a photographer from our local newspaper came to the bar to do a story on us. She asked if any of the dancers had a Christmas outfit so she could take some pictures for the paper. Since it was still almost five weeks or so until the holidays, I knew many of the girls wouldn't have anything like that at work. She asked me if I happened to have a Christmas dress and I told her I did, but it was at home. Then she asked me if I wouldn't mind posing for some pictures if she returned the next day. I agreed.

At the end of the week, the picture came out and it ended up being on the front cover of the paper! There was a great little write-up and the picture was very nice and classy. A couple men, however, had written into the paper slamming us by saying the money is dirty and the hamper society shouldn't accept it. I couldn't believe one of the writers had even commented as to why the newspaper put a photo of a server on the front cover of our local paper. People in the community, as well as staff and customers, were irate!

Rebuttal letters flooded the paper and it was wonderful to see how many women, as well as men, were on our side commenting how grateful they are that our business goes to the trouble of putting on this event every year and raising as much money as we do. Every single dancer and staff member works for free all day to try and raise as much money as possible for this important cause.

Many Big Misconceptions People Have

So, here it is. Some reasoning on the importance of strip bars and why men and women like to go. The number one reason why strip bars exist is to make money. The number one reason why men love to go to strip bars is naked women. Put the two together and you got a strip bar who employs naked women so they make money! It's all really very simple.

Probably the biggest misconception women have about strip bars is that they could steer their man to infidelity, ruining relationships and families. This is far from the truth. Men are visually stimulated and the reason the strip bar is there is to make money, not ruin relationships. It's all about business. It is the same reason dancers and staff is there as well. It comes down to cold hard cash.

This may come as a shock to many people (men and women), but the dancers and the servers don't want to sleep with your man. Hell, if we want sex, we are quite capable of finding our own partner and most of us already have. It basically comes down to us wanting to milk your man of all his money and send him home. It's nothing personal, just business.

As far as I'm concerned, if my husband were out with a bunch of friends, I would prefer him to go to a strip bar and not a normal bar or nightclub. The normal bars have the women out carousing and looking to snag a man. They'll even hit on the married ones and they don't care.

Women cringe at the thought of their man sitting at gyno, throwing money at beautiful naked girls. The reason why they throw money at them is that they love the attention they get from the women. When they receive the attention, they may be fantasizing that one of the strippers will leave with them. More upsetting is the thought of hot-looking women, possibly waving their boobs right in your man's face.

The reason the girls do it is to take their money! Men love looking at other naked women because they are visual and they can't help themselves by looking at women's bodies. What do you think happens when your guy is at the beach, on the street, at work, at the gym, or watching a movie on TV? You can't get away from hot girls; they're everywhere! Why do you think there are cheerleaders at football games or card girls at boxing matches? Why does Snap on Tools put together a calendar with beautiful women in bikinis? Did you ever notice the hot girl straddling a beautiful bike on the cover of a motorcycle magazine? I sure do … it's on my coffee table right now!

When I used to model, I got hired by a company who sold some kind of part or engine for their industry people. There was a trade fair in Portland, Oregon, and I got hired for two days to go and stand in front of their booth. My job was to say 'hello' to everyone who walked by and ask people (99 percent of them being men) if I could pin a button (advertising the company I was working for) on their jacket or shirt. Everyone said 'yes' and I even had guys come to the booth and ask, "I heard you were pinning buttons on people. Could you pin one on me as well?" It was an ingenious marketing plan! While I took a moment and did the pinning, the vultures would swoop in and start up a conversation with the potential and hopefully future "client."

If there's a hot-looking girl, of course a guy is going to look at her. Be realistic. When you notice a good-looking guy, you have a second or third look, correct? My husband knows I have the hots for David Beckham, Johnny Depp and Hugh Jackman. He doesn't get upset I take a little longer look at them than normal. It's like admiring beautiful shoes in a shoe store window.

Dancers don't want to drag your guy in the back and screw his brains out. I got some crazy news for you girlfriend, but many of the girls have their own men at home. Let me tell you that some of their guys are pretty hot!

As I've said before, the strip bar is there to make lots of money. They are there catering to men's fantasies. When looking into what other strip bars offer around the world, I found some interesting information. Some have a built in escort service (found in Europe only), themed rooms to stay in, restaurants, six girls on stage at one time, girls bathing themselves or girls swinging together in a choreographed laser show. Some strip bars don't even serve alcohol! Others have couch dances, lap dances, private dances and even bed dances. Others show off the entertainer's aerobic feats.

Did you know the biggest strip club in the world is 'The Sapphire Gentlemen's club' in Las Vegas, Nevada? It is open 24 hours a day, 7 days a week, and 365 days a year! The size of the place is 70,000 square feet and employs 8,000 exotic dancers.

Once in a while, someone will ask me why I think there are no strip bars where women hang out on a daily basis. My answer, "There are no strip bars for women, because the bar would go broke!" Women don't think about sex 24 hours a day, like most men do.

I read on the internet and found there is double the amount of women looking for employment in 2009 (the year the economy went 'wonky') compared to the year before and many of those women were looking into stripping. Strip club dancers and managers said they're drawing in the same amount of customers but very few high rollers. This industry is recession-resistant, therefore dancing = job security for the girls.

"In any moment of decision the best thing you can do is the right thing,
The next best thing is the wrong thing,
And the worst thing you can do is nothing."
- Theodore Roosevelt

www.howtobeawaitress.com

About the Author

Romana Van Lissum has been a successful cocktail waitress for over 20 years in the bar industry. Starting as a beer barrel and shooter girl in a local nightclub, she eventually got employment in a strip bar close to her home as a shooter girl. After she worked her way up to senior server, she has shared these same tips and tricks with new girls she trains that were hired for the bar. It is an industry Romana is well established in and well known.

Over the years, head-hunters would frequent the bar and offer her jobs in their bars and pubs. But as a very loyal employee, she enjoys the people she works with and serves.

In her spare time, Romana enjoys endurance riding with her horses and spending time with friends and family. She has a passion for hot yoga and meditation. You will find her in the Okanogan with her husband and dogs living out of their RV every summer for two weeks. She also loves to travel every year to the Caribbean and Las Vegas with her husband and friends.

She is a big advocate for the well being of all animals and looking after our planet earth is close to her heart.

www.howtobeawaitress.com

Made in the USA
Las Vegas, NV
06 August 2021